LATTER-DAY
WOMAN AT THE WELL

NIKKI YASTE

SNOWY PEAKS
MEDIA

CONTENTS

INTRODUCTION

My name is Nikki Yaste, although you may know me as the LDS Woman at the Well, my little piece of the internet. I blog about my transformation from self-destruction to self-discovery in Christ, my ongoing conversion to The Church of Jesus Christ of Latter-day Saints, and my daily successes and struggles.

I have traveled down a tough road. Some of it was a direct result from the choices I made. In other cases, the choices were stolen from me. I've spent a majority of my life angry and so full of anxiety that I didn't think I would ever find peace, and definitely not the peace *"which passeth all understanding." (Philippians 4:7)*

As a convert, I never had the opportunity to go to seminary. I have never been on a mission. All I really have is a transformation and a testimony. I love Christ and my Heavenly Father and I just can't stop talking about it. We are not perfect individuals and I have given up trying to become one. I prefer to let the Atonement of Christ shine through my brokenness to light up my path in front of me.

> **All I really have is a transformation and a testimony.**

For a while, I held onto my painful past like a guarded secret and played my cards close to my chest. But I realized by doing that, I wasn't fully sharing the gift that I have been given with the Atonement. If nothing else, I wanted people to see that God isn't afraid of our mess. Yes, I grew up in fear, but that doesn't mean that I am still living in fear. Yes, I made mistakes, but I am not a mistake.

i

I fell into blogging almost by accident. Even though I was baptized in 2009, I will admit that I didn't truly convert until 2013, four years after I entered into the baptismal font. When my conversion started to take shape, my life followed suit, including my conversations.

I began by posting on my social media pages what I was learning and experiencing through my scripture studies and daily life. I wrote about my struggles, my budding testimony, my heartaches, my confusion and frustration, as well as any triumphant moments in the Gospel. I posted about unanswered and answered prayers. I even wrote about the days God seemed silent and I felt alone. Anytime I felt an impression from God, I would write about it. Around this time, I remember watching Elder Bednar encourage members to share their testimonies online by using the #ShareGoodness campaign. Inwardly I smiled—it was the first time I had ever been ahead of a trend.

In the early part of 2015 I had the privilege of connecting through social media with a popular author and blogger who suggested I take my journey off Facebook and put it into a blog. He became my friend and was the first one who really believed that I had something important to share with others. I think he may have even believed in me more than I believed in myself. Sharing something on a Facebook page is one thing, taking those thoughts and putting it onto a public blog was terrifying.

For my first blog, I opted to write an introduction to myself. I've realized this truth in my short time within the Church: we cannot be fully loved until we are fully known. We are only letting people get within arm's length of us because we live in fear of judgments and opinions. When we only give them half of us, instead of all of us, we rob each other of authentic relationships and the opportunities to truly connect and heal through our faith in Jesus Christ.

My first blog, "An Honest Testimony from a Not So Typical Mormon," was a direct result from that struggle to not cave inward.

It was, literally, two years in the making. I wrote it completely from journal entries I had written throughout the years. It was a blog about being true to yourself, your past, and your authentic journey with God. It was about embracing your entire story—the good, the bad and the ugly—and letting it be seen for what it is, a testament of the Atonement at work. For an added bonus, I decided to put pictures from my days of working in the sex industry directly on the blog to help tell the story. Initially, I was told by people to take the pictures down, but I refused. This was my story. All of it. "Honest Testimony" was just that, honest. I was hanging up my mask for good.

I posted it on a Thursday and it really didn't see movement, which wasn't a concern. I didn't expect much from it. By Sunday night, I looked at my blog and it exploded from maybe one hundred views to a thousand. I was extremely freaked out by that, but my friend talked me through it and together we watched it take off like fire. When I finally went to bed Sunday night, "Honest Testimony" was at about five thousand views, but by Monday morning it had jumped to twenty thousand. Within three days, it had reached a half million people. There are still people discovering it every day.

The alerts on my phone were constantly going off. Blog comments, Facebook messages, and emails came flooding in. It was exhilarating and horrifying at the same time. I was not prepared for the outpouring of it all. I read every single email, each heartbreaking story, and cried. One part of me considered deleting the blog; the other part felt relief. I thought I was "not typical" when it came to being a Latter-day Saint, but it turns out there are a lot of people like me, just no one talked about their struggles. I promised if I continued with my blog, I would write as honestly as I could, no matter the cost. I would be authentic with every part of my walk with Jesus and within the Church. I wasn't going to cheapen myself or my testimony by faking it so people would like me.

So I did continue, and I continued to hear more stories. My next viral post was called, "Church, Why Do We Even Care?" It came as a direct result of all the emails I received from those who had left or were less active in their Christian church, regardless of denomination, because of offense. I wanted to validate those feelings, but also shake them up—why do we care about our communities' opinion? We should be focused on God's opinion. Easier to write, harder to actually do. I was also chosen by Mormon.org to blog during their addiction recovery highlight, 12 Steps to Change, in September 2015. I talked about overcoming my addiction with pornography, and got such an emotional response that I chose to write something more in-depth that I called "Breaking Free from the Chains of Pornography." Again the stories that came flooding in were overwhelming.

I don't know if it's the correct way to blog or if there is even a right way to do it. My family, excluding my husband and son, has never been a big supporter of my faith, so when they learned of the blog, they were infuriated. There were several months where we did not speak to each other because of what I wrote. But if just one person has been brought back to Jesus, or has gotten to know Him better because of my amateur writing, I believe it is worth it.

Alma sums up my feelings perfectly:

"Behold, who can glory too much in the Lord? I cannot say the smallest part which I feel." Alma 26:16

I chose to name my blog The LDS Woman at the Well because I felt like I could relate to her. Like this woman, I had not been looking for Jesus. He came for me. Because of my past and my mistakes, I was the least likely candidate for Jesus to talk to.

The Woman at the Well—married five times and currently living with her boyfriend—was just as disenchanted with society as I was. Each relationship was supposed to provide security, comfort, and protection, and yet each of her marriages ended in death or divorce, so she didn't even bother marrying her current partner. Likewise, I was disenchanted by society. I'd gotten my hopes and expectations up with so many people, and then they always disappointed or abandoned me. Each situation in my life felt like a constant stream of letdowns, one heartbreaking, humiliating moment after the next.

Like the Woman at the Well, I was thirsty. I needed that living water to finally satisfy my deepest longing—to be fully loved and accepted. I felt Christ calling me out on my actions and behaviors and prompting me to change and surrender all to Him. I knew that He could make my life greater than I ever could.

The redemptive part about the Woman at the Well's story is her willingness to accept the Gospel and teach it to those around her. She didn't know the scriptures inside and out. She had no formal training and no lifetime of experience to draw from. She used her life and her conversion to teach others, which is also the only thing that I have to offer.

My Patriarchal Blessing states many things, but the most compelling and powerful statement is, "You are called to proclaim the Gospel. You are a missionary." I hope to fulfill that call of a lifetime. It's a full-time job, but I hear the retirement plan is worth it.

Everyone has a story that can strengthen and inspire those around him or her. God is the Master Storyteller. He uses stories to change us. He builds our testimony with one small chapter, one small trial, and one small triumph at a time. There is perfect beauty in our tattered and scarred history, even if it's nothing more than the light that reflects off our mortal and broken stories. I hope that my story inspires others to see that they, too, are beloved Sons and Daughters of God. I hope to help people understand that you don't need to look a certain way to find your place within His Church. I hope you will join me in finding the living water, together, as Latter-day Women and Men at the Well.

> **Everyone has a story that can strengthen and inspire those around him or her.**

WE ARE NOT OUR CIRCUMSTANCES

"Then saith the woman of Samaria unto him, How is it that thou, being a Jew, askest drink of me, which am a woman of Samaria? For the Jews have no dealings with the Samaritans...Jesus saith unto her, Go, call thy husband, and come hither. The woman answered and said, I have no husband. Jesus said unto her, Thou hast well said, I have no husband: For thou hast had five husbands; and he whom thou hast is not thy husband: in that saidst thou truly. The woman saith unto him, Sir, I perceive that thou art a prophet." (John 4:9, 15–19)

WE DON'T ALWAYS GET WHAT WE WANT. THE CARDS WE ARE DEALT is the hand that we must play. The Woman at the Well is a woman who had a rough life, and in her first encounter with this Jewish man, there is one unavoidable fact this woman states—she's from Samaria. She didn't ask to be a Samaritan, it wasn't her sins that made her a Samaritan; it just was. As a result of something that wasn't her fault, this Samaritan woman had to deal with a lot of prejudice. She was told her place in society, and that idea was reinforced continually until she no longer saw it appropriate for a Jewish man to acknowledge her.

Second, we can speculate that she was an outcast among her own peers. Why did she have five husbands? That fact, however, may have been caused by the unfortunate choices she had made in her life.

I love that Jesus doesn't beat around the bush with her. He gently engages her, allows her the opportunity to come to Him authentically, and when she hesitates, He lovingly speaks right to the depth of her insecurities, "Sister, you are looking for love in all the wrong places." It's almost too much for her to take. I wonder if she gave him a sideways glance and smirked,

"Sir, I perceive that you are a prophet."

She is a woman who had gone down many avenues looking for love and fulfillment, and she had come up empty. She was a woman who was lost, but it ended up being worth the long journey to meet the Savior. And that day, under the hot sun, He would be the last road she would have to travel looking for that love and security. She is more than her mistakes, and her circumstances do not define her. In return, Jesus made her His first missionary.

I relate to this woman. Sometimes I think that people only read my blog because they're interested in the "car wreck." Sometimes, I believe there is a genuine interest in a world that may be foreign to them. Most times, I think people are hurting. They are frustrated with a life that may not have gone the way they wanted, but here they are. They want to relate to someone. Whatever the reason, together we are arriving at Jacob's Well, and despite all circumstances or even reasoning, Jesus is waiting for us.

I too have lived through circumstances that I did not choose for myself, and some circumstances that, unfortunately, I did choose. However, the eyes of Heaven see us for what we are, not for what we have been—a gift of grace that I am eternally grateful for.

I wasn't always known as Nikki. My birth name is Amanda Nicole, and until the age of twelve, I was known as Amanda. My home was on Caswell Drive in Orlando, Florida, right in the heart of the city. With its paneled walls and linoleum floors, we were the average American family.

I was the firstborn in my family, and therefore, incredibly spoiled. I had a bedroom filled with toys and books, a closest of frilly pink dresses and saddle shoes that I always hated. We took summer vacations to the beach, community baseball games, and visits with my grandparents. I was a happy child.

Though my mother would dote on me, dressing me up as a little doll and parading me around the house, I have always been a daddy's girl. My earliest memories are of my father with a cigarette in his mouth, strumming on his guitar, plucking out classics like Eric Clapton and Bob Dylan. He would sing "Sugar Mountain" by Neil Young, and later, when I learned the words, he would have me sing while he played. Most mornings, my father was the one to get me up and ready for preschool. It became a tradition to stop by Dunkin' Donuts for his morning coffee and a doughnut with pink sprinkles for me.

Despite the many happy times in the early years of my childhood, there was a storm brewing beneath the surface of Caswell Drive. My parents began to argue a lot. At first, they tried to keep me out of their arguments, but they argued so often that it became my new normal. When they weren't arguing I felt anxious. I began to find comfort in their fighting. Between the verbal assaults and threats of divorce, I would be lulled to sleep as if by a music box.

The problems at home began to manifest themselves in other ways. I attended a Lutheran preschool and kindergarten academy and was often slapped with rulers for misbehaving. When you think of a mean, bully child, I'm horrified to admit that was me. I would find the weakest kid in my class and tease that child relentlessly. I was always fighting with the other children or bossing them around. For a five-year-old, I was awful and I knew it. I adopted the vulgar language my parents used in our home and yelled it across playgrounds and classrooms to other children. I practically took out real estate in "time out."

On one particular afternoon, I was sitting in the living room coloring and watching cartoons while listening to my parents argue in the garage. The argument moved inside the house, slamming doors along the way. I remember them standing beside me screaming at each other. Then my father, in his rage, pushed my mother over the side of the couch and started choking her. Absolutely terrified, I stood and just stared down at them. I can still see my father's hands around my mother's neck as she screamed for me to get help and call 911. I had never seen my father raise his hands to my mother before that moment, but it was like he snapped. I can still see the veins in his neck and hear him as he screamed for my mother to shut up.

I called out to my father and, as if being pulled from a trance, he took one look at me, crawled off my mother and walked outside, slamming the door behind him. I was so scared that I just stood there shaking violently as I watched my mother try, and fail, to collect herself. My father moved out shortly after, claiming it was "better to have two happy homes than one miserable one," and left my sister and me with my mother.

After he moved out, Dad and Mom managed to maintain a decent correspondence in those initial months of separation, and we saw him often. But my mother, ever the expert at moving forward in life, quickly found herself a new boyfriend, Ed, who was a single father with a young daughter, Tina. Though I don't remember Mom ever referring to Ed as her "boyfriend," I do remember going over to Ed's house for hours while Tina, Alisha, and I awkwardly sat on the couch and watched cartoons.

Everything was okay until Dad found himself a new girlfriend, Pam—nine years Mom's junior. My mom went ballistic, so insane with jealousy and rage that she quickly married Ed. It felt as if one day we were just visiting Ed, and the next he was moving in with his daughter and we were to call him, "Daddy Andersen," something my dad always hated.

The following year, my dad married Pam in a small ceremony. Even though my mother had remarried, she had a hard time letting go of my dad and accepting his new relationship with Pam. My father's marriage to a much younger woman made my mother insecure, so she found little ways to punish him through his children, particularly me. Often, she wouldn't tell him about school plays or award ceremonies, and because of that, my dad missed a lot of our elementary life.

I became an easy and vulnerable target for her anger because of him. I learned to dance around my mother. I could anticipate her mood swings and rearrange myself accordingly. Every little mannerism that I inherited from my dad would send her on a rollercoaster of emotion. Either she would start screaming a litany of abusive names because I looked like him, or she would wallow in self-pity—sending me on a guilt trip—and wanting confirmation that I loved her more than him despite what my genetics betrayed.

I wouldn't say we were poor growing up. We always had a roof over our head and at least some type of income, but my mother mismanaged the finances. She relied heavily on child support, though my sister and I hardly saw any of that money. We wore second-hand clothing and worn out shoes. The kitchen cabinets always seemed bare of anything of value. I remember plenty of meals being a can of vegetables or Lay's potato chips with melted shredded cheese.

In my mother's defense, she hated to cook and so she hardly ever did. She was just as content to drive through Taco Bell and order as many tacos as she could to get through the week. As young kids, we loved it. It was much better than a heated up can of peas or microwaved eggs in a coffee cup.

The more and more my mother complained about my dad, the more I got used to her rants. They became the soundtrack of my childhood. One morning, I was sitting in front of the TV watching my cartoons and eating breakfast at the coffee table. My mother once again began to scream and accuse my father of being a "deadbeat dad." Sensing we had finally stopped listening to her, her complaining became violent.

I must have given her a look, or maybe it was my lack of attention that set her off, but she lunged at me, pulling my hair and slapping me in the head and face. In between her smacks, she screamed that I made her sick, that I had ruined her life and if given the option she would get rid of me. I was in the third grade and I can still remember it like it was just happening. I begged her to stop, screaming that she was hurting me. I pleaded with her to let go of my hair. I think we were trying to out scream each other because the louder I got from the pain, the louder she became trying to drown me out.

Eventually she let go, but the abuse was already done. When she stepped back to survey her damage, even she was in shock. She retreated to her bedroom in tears.

And that's when our new routine started. My mother would bash on me and then exit to her bedroom to wallow in self-pity. The abuse over the years became extreme and frequent. We would be driving down the road, I'd look at her a certain way and she'd slam my head against the window. I would be pushed down stairs or thrown against doors for simply being in her way. I had objects thrown at me, like a ceramic mug that collided with my head during one of her rants. There were several times I was forced to stay home from school because of the evidence she left all over my body. I lived in fear of my mother. She dictated the mood of that house. I walked on eggshells so much I built callouses on my nine-year-old feet. She would start screaming and I would have moved the earth and moon if it meant she would just stop yelling and be happy for once.

Here's the strange dynamic of a child that is being abused—I always felt like I deserved what I had coming to me. I felt like I was the product of all her misery. I was, after all, my father's daughter. After an abusive episode, my mother would hole off in her room where eventually I would shamefully make my way there and *apologize* to her for making her mad.

I would start the reconfirming dance I always did.

"I love you more than dad. I want to live with you. You are better than my father."

There would be a few tender moments as she would dote on me, but it never lasted. As a young child, I loved my mother, but I was never comfortable around her. I felt like a stranger. Someone on the outside looking in on a life that I wasn't supposed to have.

We don't always get what we want, but we get what we get. There are many of us that carry a cross we didn't ask for and we certainly didn't expect. If we don't learn to transform our pain through Christ, we will transfer it on to future generations. My mother came from an abusive background, as did her mother before her. Those behaviors and reactions to anger were bred throughout my lineage. It's a knee-jerk response to what we know, but it's wrong and it's damaging.

It's only been through the love and grace I have received from Jesus Christ that has allowed me to break that generational chain and cycle of abuse. It has removed that fear and shame associated with those types of behaviors.

If we don't learn to transform our pain through Christ, we will transfer it on to future generations.

We are not defined by our circumstances. We are called to come out of what keeps us chained to the enemy's lies—that we deserved it, that we are unworthy, that we will never outrun it. It's a courageous existence to allow yourself to live beyond that which we think defines us and rely on God. Only living within the gospel has made me that brave. Only developing an intimate relationship with Jesus has allowed me to take what He says at face value.

It boils down to this: abuse is never okay. No, you do not and did not deserve it. Yes, you deserve to be loved, cherished, and protected.

Everything within the gospel shows us that Jesus is on the side of the oppressed, not the oppressor. He came to be crushed and bruised with those who have been crushed and bruised. Where is God when it hurts? He is found in one that is hurting, not the one that does the hurting. My mother may have inflicted a lot of damage in my childhood, but God did not. Our Savior kneels down, looks us right in the eye, and tenderly bandages our cuts and bruises. We are not just healed by the Savior—we are made whole.

When I was little, I wanted to be better for my mom, but I could never figure out how to make her happy. I decided at a young age that I would be a "good girl." I toed the line, tried to appease my mother, not ask any questions or challenge her, and tried to predict her ever-changing mood. Unfortunately, living that way made me incredibly insecure and withdrawn from my peers. When I was in sixth grade, my father began taking me to a child therapist who, bless his heart, tried to coax me out of my shell. Unfortunately, I was too scared of saying something that might get my mother in trouble, so I holed up inside myself and answered his questions accordingly.

On February 12, 1997, I had my last appointment with the therapist. The night before, my mother had come home from work to find her laundry not folded to her liking. She beat me so bad that no matter what I could have done to salvage that situation in her favor, my face revealed the evidence. By my swollen lips and from the doctor's intuition, Child Services was called and I was placed into my father's care. I was twelve years old. I remember the date like I remember my anniversary. That memory is seared in me forever.

It was traumatic watching my mother scream and cry like a wounded animal, on her knees begging me not to go as I packed up my clothing in a small suitcase. I felt like I had betrayed her and that after this, she would definitely have a hard time loving me. It was awful. For a split second I almost asked to stay with her, but I didn't.

A few days later, after the emotional embers cooled, my father drove me to my mother's home to retrieve the last of my belongings. I found some of my things in a black trash bag by the door. Everything else of mine had been thrown away; my room was transformed into my sister's bedroom, complete with new furniture and clothing that wasn't bought at the Salvation Army. My father was furious. I just cried.

Sometimes I wonder what it would have been like if I'd stayed with my mother. How would I have turned out? Would I have made different decisions? Maybe I would have been a runaway. Maybe I would have turned out the exact same way I am today. I don't know. But, looking back at the details, I do believe that God had a plan for me from the very beginning. The scriptures say,

> *"Before I formed thee I knew thee; and before thou camest forth out of the womb I sanctified thee." (Jeremiah 1:5)*

God knew what I would be up against, and yet He called and qualified me to do it. I have this visual of me in the premortal existence, probably in ripped jeans and flannel raising my hand for the assignment. It's been a heavy burden, but through the gospel, I have been able to unload some of that baggage where it matters most—at the foot of the cross.

I have forgiven my mother for the mistakes she made and have let go of my anger and resentment, though the journey has not been an easy one. There are times she can be vindictive and manipulative. Currently, there are no pictures of me or my family hanging in her home. But for all my mother's flaws, she can be loving and very funny. I can call her for advice or a complaint. Sometimes I see her more like a friend than a mother to me and that's ok. I love her for who she is and not for what I think she should be. I also believe, in the end, God is true to His promises. The relationships that I want now will one day be fulfilled, and I look forward to that restoration.

I left my mother's house with my childhood in a garbage bag and began the next phase in God's plan by moving in with my father. My dad, determined to support me in a fresh start, suggested that I change my name.

"I always really liked your middle name, Nicole. How about you go by Nikki?"

And so, from that moment on, I was no longer Amanda. I was Nikki.

The dynamic of my father's home versus my mother's was a strange one. Even though she was abusive, she was very relaxed with

I left my mother's house with my childhood in a garbage bag

9

her rules. We didn't have a bedtime. She hardly checked our homework. There was very little routine or predictability. My mother was not above packing us up and taking us to a hotel on a school night just because she felt like getting out of the house.

My father's house was very traditional and very routine, which I found comfort in. At my mother's, we spent the weekends walking around the mall or sneaking into hotel pools to go swimming. At my father's, we spent the weekends at home where he did little fix-up projects around the house. My stepmother, Pam, always cooked, and we ate dinners around the table every night. We all had to be there, no exceptions.

I think my father wasn't sure what to do with this awkward, damaged young girl. The first thing Dad and Pam did was buy me new clothing for my fresh start at my new school in the middle of my sixth grade year. They took me to JCPenny's and I felt like a princess. I remember they bought me these adorable polo shirts, from back when people thought wearing polo outside of golf memberships were cool, and Nike tennis shoes. I was stoked for those shoes. I kept the box they came in for years as a memento. I felt so cool.

Unfortunately, living with my mom had made me insecure and awkward. Also, I was overweight from years of not eating properly. I had buck teeth and out-of-style hair, and I was a head taller than most of my classmates.

I entered into middle school on the loser side of life. I was picked on—a lot—and I had few friends.

At home, my dad and stepmom decided to try and pretty me up. I think this is where I adopted the "skinny blonde" mentality as the ideal for beauty. Both my mother and Pam were tiny blonde women, and if you could tell by my description, I was not. My dad took me straight to an orthodontist to fix my teeth with braces. Unfortunately, we hit a roadblock; I needed to wait until my wisdom teeth came in. My father, the driven man he is, found another way. I could have surgery and get them removed early, so I did. However, the drawback to that is that for the rest of my life I feel pressure and pain in my mouth from simple sinus congestion. But at least my teeth were getting fixed, right?

The next thing they decided to tackle was my weight. For the first time in my life, I was encouraged to participate in sports and play outside. I joined the cheerleading squad and the volleyball team. The food I ate was monitored and there were several times I was reprimanded about going back for seconds or eating all the food on my plate. "A lady," I was told, "is to leave an extra bite oon the side of her plate." That's translation for: "Slow down, fatty." And thus began my love/hate relationship with food.

I learned it was a lot easier to fall asleep than to deal with the hunger pains, so I did. Later, when I told Pam about my newly found weight loss technique, I was praised for it. I had found my niche *and* I was losing weight! So, instead of valuing intelligence, I leaned heavily on my looks well into my twenties.

My father came from a military background; therefore, he was very strict and very demanding. He expected a lot from me and I wasn't allowed to show emotion. Ever. He was extremely critical and condescending and often as a teenager, I would be left in tears as he berated me over a simple mistake I had made, and then berated me again because I dared to be emotional. He had a specific plan that he wanted for my life and I was to color inside the lines without question. I learned to push down my emotions and project what my father expected from me. By the time I was a young adult, I was an expert at becoming whatever *anyone* wanted me to be.

As a young girl coming from my mother's abusive environment, I didn't respond to his "tough love" in a healthy way. It made me overly sensitive and extremely hard on myself. I could never accept a compliment—I would always try and balance it out with something negative. If someone told me, "You did a great job, Nikki," I needed to add a "but I could have…" I learned that from my father, who was the ultimate compliment balancer. I could always do things better.

Every idea I had, everything I wanted to be, in his eyes, was just the fantasy of a teenager. I grew up to have a very cynical view of myself.

My mother was absent for most of my early teenage years. She never called or came to visit me. The responsibility to maintain a relationship with her landed completely on my shoulders. There were many nights where I would wait for a phone call that did not come or a visit that would be cancelled. I learned to anticipate my mother disappointing me. Now that I know the custody arrangements, I have a clearer understanding of why things were that way, though it doesn't excuse her behavior. I was my father's responsibility and my sister was my mother's. The contact only needed to be minimal. When I turned sixteen and started to drive, we started to have a relationship because I could put in the effort to see her, which I did as often as I could.

I think Pam eventually grew tired of me being in her house. I learned long afterward that my arrangements to live with my dad were supposed to be temporary until my mom got the help she needed. However, within a month, my mother signed over all her parental rights and I became a permanent member in my father's home.

Pam had a hard time adjusting to this very broken preteen girl that suddenly lived there full time instead of just every other weekend. She didn't know how to be a mother to me and I think she felt a lot of pressure, especially since my own mother had thrown in the towel. Also, although he was hard on me, being my dad's biological daughter meant there was still that genetic connection that my dad just didn't have with her two daughters, and that bothered her.

To make an effort to appease her, Dad began to spend less time with me and more time with her girls or all of us together. That was tough. Her daughters would get special treatment that I didn't receive in an effort to maintain some type of peace. What my father didn't know was that I was slowly feeling the divide between myself and everyone else in my family.

I was fourteen when my parents decided that I needed to learn the value of a dollar. They sat me down at the dining room table and informed me of my new responsibility to find a job immediately. That same pressure to "pay your own way" was not applied to Pam's eldest daughter when she turned fourteen two years later.

We lived in a pretty rural area, so any job was about thirty minutes away. My parents drove me to the middle of town, dropped me off, and told me to get to work. I walked those streets applying for jobs over and over again, only to be turned down because of my age. Fortunately, I found a job at Winn-Dixie, a grocery store, bagging groceries and stocking shelves. I had to wait a few weeks until I turned fifteen to actually start, but I got a real job where I could earn real money.

With the job came a newfound sense of adulthood. In small decisions that I made for myself, I gradually began rebelling against my dad's "inside-the-lines" plan that he had laid out for me. I started gaining attention from my older coworkers, and even boys.

I went on my first date when I was fifteen years old. I didn't know about living prophets who had counseled youth not to date until sixteen, but I can tell you from experience that it is wise counsel, as is all of their guidance to teenagers. I ended up accompanying a senior boy, Troy, to his prom. I was not into Troy, but my dad liked him a lot. Troy was built like an ox. He played varsity football and I thought he was dumb. In an effort to impress me, he would come over and help my dad with projects in the yard. My dad almost offered a dowry.

When he asked me to prom, my parents were thrilled. I wasn't interested and didn't want to go, but my parents insisted it would be good for me, so I went. I tried to avoid him most of the night. Later, when he drove me home, he tried to kiss and grope me. I stopped him and told him, "Thanks, but no thanks." He laughed and tried again. This time, I was more firm and slapped his hands away. Troy lost it. He started banging on the steering wheel and screaming at me for being a tease. He practically pushed me out of his truck. He left me standing outside in my front yard shaking.

After that moment, I kind of stopped investing in humanity. I felt like I had gotten the short end of the stick when it came to life. I decided that the world was made up of either victims or bullies, and I was done being a victim. I questioned whether I had ever been loved. Was it possible that there was any love in the relationships with my abusive mother, my military father, my inconvenienced stepmother, the boys who seemed to only want one thing from me? Mostly, I thought God, if there even was a God, was a sadist.

The years have shined a different light on that shaking, scared fifteen-year-old girl. I have realized that there was love in those relationships, though it was imperfect because imperfect people expressed it. However, I know—and if you put the book down at this point and don't read another chapter, I want you to know—God does love me and He does love you. And it's not in His own way; there is only one way that He loves, and it's in a perfect way. Looking back through those broken times I can see His hand comforting me, preparing me, and teaching me. I can see where He called out to me, but at that time I did not know my shepherd's voice.

> **If you put the book down ... and don't read another chapter, I want you to know— God does love me and He does love you.**

Wherever you are, whoever you are, whatever you've done, God loves you. Don't fight against Him. Don't put effort into convincing yourself that He doesn't exist or that He doesn't care. Life's hard enough. Don't turn your back on your one constant ally.

Does an unwavering belief mean that you won't have trials? That's not what the scriptures say. In fact, this experience from Joseph Smith, a man who always tried to be his best through trials and torture, shows that trials come to everyone. He asked in one of the low moments of his life:

"O God, where art thou? And where is the pavilion that covereth thy hiding place? How long shall thy hand be stayed, and thine eye,

yea thy pure eye, behold from the eternal heavens the wrongs of thy people and of thy servants, and thine ear be penetrated with their cries?" (D&C 121: 1–2)

God lovingly told him as He tells us:

"Peace be unto thy soul; thine adversity and thine afflictions shall be but a small moment; And then, if thou endure it well, God shall exalt thee on high." (D&C 121:7)

Although our circumstances may not be what we choose, the Lord has qualified us for them. He will help us through them, and He promises that it will only be a small moment.

LOOKING FOR LIVING WATER IN ALL THE WRONG PLACES

"Jesus answered...If thou knewest the gift of God, and who it is that saith to thee, Give me to drink; thou wouldest have asked of him, and he would have given thee living water. The woman saith unto him, Sir, thou hast nothing to draw with, and the well is deep; from whence then hast thou that living water? Jesus answered...Whosoever drinketh of the water that I shall give him shall never thirst; but the water that I shall give him shall be in him a well of water springing up into everlasting life. The woman saith unto him, Sir give me this water, that I thirst not, neither come hither to draw." (John 4: 10–15)

INITIALLY WHEN CHRIST TELLS THE WOMAN OF THE LIVING WATER HE IS offering her, she immediately thought it was a physical and natural element that sprang from the earth. It's also interesting to note that she points out, probably sarcastically, that Jesus lacks the one thing to carry the water—a bucket. When we chase after the things of the world, we will always need something else to help satisfy us. Physical water is great, but to actually retrieve that water successfully, you will need a bucket. To gain praise from man is great, but to maintain that praise you will have to conform and perform.

It is only the living water that flows from Jesus Christ that can fill, heal, and restore us, and we will never need anything more than that. It will always be enough for us. If we insist on chasing after other waters that only temporarily satisfy us, we only end up discouraged, disheartened, tired, and looking for something more. We will never have a big enough bucket.

Despite what brought you to Jacob's well, we are not our circumstances or mistakes. However, it would be naïve to say that our upbringing, whether good or bad, does not influence our decisions in our everyday life. They paint a picture of how we see the world around us, other people, and ourselves. While there were many moments in my life when I was forced to react and adapt to my surroundings, there were other times that I chose to act irresponsibly and dangerously.

When I began to understand the life of the Savior, not once did I ever look at His life and think He was missing out on something. When I lined my party lifestyle up to Jesus, it was me who came up short and was found wanting. I knew I was missing out on something. What He had, I desperately needed, though I had to drop my bucket a few more times into the well to realize that.

From the moment I was hired by Winn Dixie, I paid for everything myself. I found comfort and a social life at work, which is where I made many older friends. I liked earning money, but most of all, working gave me the independence and social life I desperately craved, and I got it on my own terms. I was a completely different person around my friends. I felt validated and appreciated at work, while at home I tended to blend into the scenery and became a recluse. Having a job really brought out those teen angst years in me. I hated being home.

My family, especially my dad, didn't understand me, but my older and fellow outcast friends did. Everyone had cooler parents or lived with roommates, and they never called me fat or made me feel worthless. I felt a lot of anger toward my family. When I was home, I would hide in my room and listen to music, write poetry, and count down the days until I could move out and finally be free. See, I told you—teen angst to the fullest. The more my father pushed me, the further it pushed me away.

Parents, if we do not validate our children with words of affirmation and compassion, someone else will. Someone more destructive and harmful to your children. If we do not teach them their identity as a son or daughter of God, the world will come along and give them one. The abuse with my mother led to deep-rooted insecurities. The pressure to live up to some unattainable standard with my dad only reconfirmed those insecurities, and I gave them life. My friends, insecure and deeply troubled themselves, came along and fed me what I needed to hear: you are worthy; you are important; you are loved.

Sure, I was loved, worthy, and important for all the wrong reasons—but at least they were proud of me. Most of my bad decisions, if not all, can be traced back to being with the wrong people who made me feel the right things. This is when I started to first experiment with the party scene, and I found that I really fit in there, or so I thought. The problem was, because I started building my identity on my friends, when those relationships went sour—and most of them did—so did my sense of self, and I wound up even more lost and rejected.

> **Most of my bad decisions, if not all, can be traced back to being with the wrong people who made me feel the right things.**

I learned to be a really good liar. With my family, I abided by the rules and kept to myself. But when I went out, I would call my parents from one friend's house or from a pay phone to confirm I was there, only to hang up and be out the door, never to be seen the rest of the night. I learned what time my parents went to bed so I could sneak out of the house.

With my friends, I was loud and outgoing. I was adventurous and willing to try anything once. I realize now how dangerous it was to have zero accountability for our whereabouts. I've put myself into a lot of questionable situations for the sake of a "good time."

By the time I turned seventeen, I really just lived for the weekend. Everything revolved around getting drunk and being with my friends. I wore different clothing underneath my conservative, family-approved attire. My best friend, Emily, and I were attached at the hip. We did everything together. We would sneak into bars, underage, and try to get as many guys as we could to buy us drinks. She encouraged me to come out of my shell a little more and embrace life as it came to me.

Emily and I developed a motto that became the theme of our lives: *"You only get a dollar."* We meant it in context of life—life was like a dollar, once you spend it, it's gone, so it's best if you live it up. I remember saying to myself a lot, "You only get a dollar, just do it." Was it eloquent? No, but it was enough to rationalize guilty feelings and justify bad decisions.

This was the age that I learned how to manipulate men to get what I wanted. It started with small things, like a ride or food. Eventually, I manipulated them to get alcohol or money. I used men to my advantage, and in hindsight, they probably used me as well.

It was that polluted thinking that made it a lot easier to start to hustle random men for things my meager paychecks couldn't afford. I had an insatiable need for attention, and I used my wardrobe and mannerisms to get it. I drank so much in those years—I drank to fit in and then I drank to cope and forget. What started as just a few forbidden sips turned into stealing alcohol and persuading people to buy it for me since I was still underage.

Drinking became a big problem for me. I'd be late or miss work completely because I was still too drunk or hung over to function properly. Sometimes, regrettably, I went to work still trashed from the night before. I have clear memories of waking up at a friend's home, but having zero recollection of how I got there. Did I drive? I may have hitchhiked. I don't know.

It caused a lot of problems in my social life, which was ironic because that was what brought me to drinking in the first place. I was fighting with everyone or I was becoming very promiscuous, experimenting and exploring my sexuality. I had no filter and no sense of awareness. My common sense took an extended vacation during those years. It's like that thing between my ears that God had given me—my brain—didn't work. Or maybe it did, I just learned to shut it off.

When I was invited to model nude for a friend and submit pictures to a magazine, I accepted because I wanted to. I wasn't forced. I wasn't coerced. I believed one hundred percent that what I was doing was normal and empowering as a woman.

Here is what the magazines don't show you: I prepped for hours to achieve the look I wanted. I starved for days and worked out for weeks to lose weight. I spent tons of money on hair, makeup, and beauty treatments.

I cried when I saw the pictures. I saw every flaw on my skin, every stomach roll, every scar, everything. What was supposed to be empowering only made me more insecure, especially when I compared myself to my counterparts, other gorgeous and seemingly flawless women.

But it's all a lie. What the pornography industry portrays is entirely fake, and the people involved in it harbor some deep-seated damage. Everything is over-the-top, and no one—and I mean absolutely no one—is a porn star in "real life." Pornography falls short when hit with the reality of real relationships, because as appetizing as pornography seems, it is based on a perverted view of a heavenly function of our bodies.

It's a truth that I knew, but rarely listened to. I bought into the lie and developed a full-blown eating disorder because of it. I was obsessed with the scale, pinching my sides to see if there was any evidence of excess fat, spending hours at the gym, and popping speed for weight loss. I remember days where my only food consisted of half of a bagel and a cup of yogurt and that was it. I looked like a skeleton in many of my pictures from my late teens, early twenties.

When I was in college, I really hit rock bottom, or so I thought. I attended school three hours away from my hometown. Not a huge drive, but just long enough to be excluded from many things with my friends at home. I felt lonely and depressed. I really struggled my freshman year and gained the "freshman fifteen" from drinking a lot, which also fueled my eating disorder. The weight gain and being isolated from the friends I knew made me miserable. I would try to include myself in things my home friends were doing, but making the drive all the time was hard on me and my wallet. I felt stuck. I was grateful when the summer came around and I got to go home. That summer, I really began to change. I started bleaching my hair blonde and tanning to form a new look I wanted to project. When I went back to college for my sophomore year, I was unrecognizable and I loved it.

My sophomore year, I began to date a lot and I had my first real interest in gaining a steady boyfriend instead of temporary relationships with random men. I dated a guy named Matt who was a big drinker, like myself. Matt was fun and encouraged me to live life to the fullest with no regrets. "We only have a dollar!"

My friends hated him. When I fell on hard times financially, Matt suggested that I start amateur stripping at a local club. I rationalized that since I had already modeled naked, what was the big deal? I figured it was just another party and "if God gave it to me, I might as well flaunt it."

That is the biggest lie the enemy has ever told women. The truth is, God gave you your body as a beautiful gift. It's funny that when the world hears about the law of chastity or the Word of Wisdom, it says, "Ugh, how can you live with those restrictions?" But it's that same world that wants to use and abuse and gawk at that body of yours until the alcohol, drugs, and excess start to kick in, and then they're ready to move on to the next pretty, young flaunter. God's laws make you feel better about your body, teach you how to master it, how to give it the maximum opportunity for long-term good health.

Since I had been to strip clubs before, I figured this would be easy. And I needed the money. I look back now and realize how stupid I was. There is no good explanation I can give for it that doesn't make me sound selfish and immature. I could have gone to my dad for money, but I didn't want the lecture that came with it. I didn't want to feel guilty and like a failure. I didn't want to explain why I was having financial problems. It wasn't worth it.

Dancing—and my life—took a lot out of me, mentally. I was constantly in turmoil. The long nights and early morning classes started taking their toll, so I took pills to stay awake, courtesy of another stripper. I hated what I was doing, I hated who I was becoming, and yet I couldn't stop. I knew what I was doing was wrong. I knew if my dad found out it would crush him. In that life, the lines of what was right became blurry. Though I never crossed this line, I saw several of my fellow dancers entering into the world of prostitution.

I learned to disconnect when I danced, throwing on the charm but not caring about one guy from the next. I learned to flirt my way right into a man's heart, and by heart, I mean his wallet. I lied to every single person I encountered. Every. Single. Person.

I truly believed that there was no such thing as true love. It was hard to believe in the sanctity of marriage when one of your regulars was a married man who swore he *never* did this, but of course I would see him the following week. The sad part about it is I didn't see past my own selfish needs and desires—I didn't see the family attached to some of these people; all I saw was the man attached to a wallet.

I saw a really ugly and vulnerable side to people and explored a really dark side to myself. I comforted myself with the fact that I was the one in control of the situation. It was the guy getting played, not me, and I could draw the line and cut off the situation whenever I wanted to.

My last night dancing I had the scariest encounter of my life up until that point. A client attacked and started choking me. This loss of control freaked me out so bad I immediately left the club, and I never went back.

After I quit dancing and went back to working a normal job, I didn't feel comfortable living in the area I was in knowing that some of my former clients were classmates. I needed a change, so I signed up for the military. I told myself if I got away, I could start fresh. I could get better. I could stop drinking. I could leave it all behind me. Most of my life had been spent chasing new beginnings or searching for a place I could comfortably call home.

It's hard to leave the scene of old habits and behaviors. It's a gritty decision to actively remove yourself, and it's a choice you will have to make daily. I guess I didn't have the fortitude at that time. I stopped dancing, sure, but I started dating a guy who was in and out of jail because of DUI's that he collected like people collect stamps.

> **It's hard to leave the scene of old habits and behaviors... and it's a choice you will have to make daily.**

Accepting calls from the county jailhouse weren't my proudest moments. Of course, those DUI's didn't slow down his drinking, only his driving, so I quickly became his drinking buddy or chauffeur.

He also pushed me into really working in pornography. It was his way of trying to earn a quick dollar for the both of us, although I hardly saw a dime of that money. I was still trapped in the mindset of "this was okay." I rationalized that unlike dancing, in the world of cameras and lights, I had control.

Tragically, my illusion of control over my life evaporated a couple weeks before I went into basic training. I went to a party where, once again, I had too much to drink, causing me to pass out. I woke up as a man raped me. I had been unable to control what was happening and I will never forget the terror of that moment as long as I live.

I remember him saying over his shoulder as he left that I deserved it for being a drunk slut. I lay in that bed crying until I felt like I had been drained dry, and then I threw up everything that was in my stomach.

I remember feeling really angry at my parents, first for being physically and emotionally abusive and negligent, but also for not being there when I needed them, like right then. I'd always felt independent and grown up for the decisions I was making, but right then I was a weeping child calling out for any parental arms to hold me and make it better. I was afraid, exposed, vulnerable, and I was completely alone. For the first time in my life, I prayed. It wasn't elegant and it wasn't formulaic. It was simple and direct.

"God, if you exist, you're probably mad at me, but I really need you to help me."

I hated myself. I actually believed that I deserved it. I felt dirty and used and I never wanted to talk about it because I feared people would side with the guy. Surely, I had been walking in the devil's playground. If I insisted on dancing with Satan, should I really be surprised?

And the answer is yes, I should be surprised. Regardless of the circumstances that I may or may not have put myself into, no one deserves to be mistreated and violated in such a violent manner. Unless it happens to you personally, you will never know how it feels to be violated in such a way and made to feel as if you were nothing, with absolutely no worth or value. Up until that point, I felt I had the power. He stole what was only my choice and my right. When I became a Latter-day Saint I learned a higher way of thinking—that that man stole what belonged to God, but God has restored it to me, plus some.

If anyone reading has been in this position, you did not deserve it and it was not your fault, and may God judge the one who has hurt you.

The morning after, I remember it was painful to walk and I was heavily bruised, but those wounds healed in time. The real violence of a sexual crime occurs internally. It leads to years of depression, nightmares, memory loss, and sexual dysfunction.

Decades later, the suffering and pain continue. Even after I was married, I struggled to open up intimately with my husband. Most of our arguments stemmed from the behavior and abuse that I experienced *before* I even met my husband. I compared him to the men I met at the strip clubs or to this rapist. I still suffer triggers. For instance, crowds, especially people standing too close to me, can trigger something deep inside me that makes me feel like I am losing control of the situation.

Through these years I was always looking for a fresh start, a way to break out of all the bad from my life and magically transform into something new. As I'd try to gain control, I found myself deeper in situations and emotions that were overpowering.

The Savior's promise is that *"Whosoever will lose his life for my sake shall find it."* (Matthew 16:25)

My fresh start that I wanted so badly after I joined the military didn't exist until I converted to the gospel and accepted Jesus as my Savior, instead of my judge. Christ always saved his most loving and compassionate words for those who had fallen deeply into sexual sin. When Jesus looked over Jerusalem, the scriptures say He wept. I believe when He looks over those who have been broken, abused, and have not made the best decisions, He weeps for each of us individually. Our pain is not something that is abstract to Him, but something that is real and tangible. His tears are not tears of disgust or disappointment, but loving as a Father who only wants the absolute best for His children.

This is difficult to write, but that downward spiral was a defining moment for me spiritually. Even with the men who overstepped my boundaries in the past, I managed to maintain control and leave the situation. A few weeks before I left for basic training, I was the means to an end for a guy who took advantage of a defenseless and damaged woman. This time there was no out. Out of so much pain came my first real cry to God. I needed something—no, *someone*—bigger than myself to help me. I needed a Savior. Our bodies are made in the image of our Father in Heaven. We are the object of God's delight and we deserve to be treated with tenderness, love, and compassion, especially in our most intimate moments. In sex, we may engage our bodies, but unlike sneezing and coughing, when we participate in sex, it touches a person's soul—as softly and carefully as it can be touched by another human being in such a vulnerable way. It's as powerful as it is celestial. It is a gift given from God and we are to cherish it, one on one, with a person who can see it as the gift it truly is. I wish I had understood that depth and magnitude when I was younger.

It's not easy to escape sexual trauma, but if you find yourself burdened you can overcome it. There have been times I've had to lovingly tell myself that I have been set free from that bondage, the living water flows in and around me and is as protective as it is calming. I am more than what my circumstances have been.

Living the gospel demands a lot, but living "in the world" demands a lot more and it gives a lot less. The world has an insatiable appetite with standards that are impossible to meet. Unlike finding completeness in Christ, the living water, the world offers us nothing. It will never fill you permanently. You will always come up short and be found wanting. There will always be more and more that you have to do to prove yourself to others.

> **Living the gospel demands a lot, but living "in the world" demands a lot more and it gives a lot less.**

It starts out as a little fun, but eventually you will find yourself having to do more to feel that same thrill. And if you're curious about that, just ask an addict. What started out for me as a little fun with friends turned into a full-blown sex addiction that ended with me working and living within the industry and an alcohol dependency that got me fired from jobs, kicked out of bars, in with the absolute worst crowds, and a night of violence that I will never forget.

In the Book of Mormon, Nephi teaches, "*[Satan] will lull them away into carnal security, that they will say: All is well . . . and thus the devil cheateth their souls, and leadeth them away carefully down to hell.*" (2 Nephi 28:21)

I believe that scripture because I lived it. Every party, every empty bottle, every late night at bars and clubs were just evidence of me looking for the living water and something that would finally take away that thirst I had been living with. It was like I was drinking salt water and slowly dying from dehydration. I believed that everything I was doing was empowering and fun. I believed that everything was going to be okay, that everything *was* okay, because everyone seemed to be doing what I was doing. The reality is, no, everyone is not drinking and living promiscuously; only the people that I was determined to surround myself with were.

Leading someone down to hell is a gradual slope, but Satan has a plan to get you there. Satan is carefully crafting our downfall, so we must be stronger. I know that stripping and pornography are not the path most Latter-day Saints take, but I choose to share my story to stop it from becoming the way for just one other Latter-day Saint. The reality is, this brutal side of life has affected and is affecting some of us. Sometimes we shy away from these ugly topics. I know it is as hard for some of you to hear about as it is for me to share it. I take inspiration from Paul and Alma, who not only abandoned their sinful ways of life, but used their experiences to stop others from falling into those same situations. This does not have to be someone else's story.

In 3 Nephi 17, Jesus asks the Nephites to bring those who are sick to Him for healing. He says,

> "*Have you any that are sick among you? Bring them hither. Have ye that are lame, or blind, or halt, or maimed, or leprous, or that*

are withered, or that are deaf, or are afflicted in any manner? Bring them hither and I will heal them, for I have compassion upon you." (3 Nephi 17: 7, emphasis added)

I love that. I love that Jesus takes the time to not just name physical ailments, but calls those who *"are afflicted in any manner"*—He is taking the time to call all those who have been wounded emotionally, spiritually, and mentally as well. He cares deeply for all of us. Until you have walked in a person's shoes, the truth is you don't know how it feels. You can't understand what it means to be exploited, objectified, raped, abused, and even if those terrifying words can be applied to you, we all process it differently. But, no matter what condition or circumstance we may find ourselves in, Jesus Christ is personally invested in every single one of us. I don't know how He does it, but for now, I can take comfort in the fact that He does. The Atonement is universal, but it is applied individually to each of our sins and pains.

The first time I read and truly understood 1 Corinthians 6:20, I cried: *"For ye are bought with a price: therefore glorify God in your body, and in your spirit, which are God's."*

As someone who sold herself for pleasure, this hit me in the stomach and took my breath away. First, it meant that I had a price. I wasn't junk or worthless. I had value and Jesus, the Savior of the World, saw that value and paid the final price for someone like me. Someone like you. He didn't just ransom my sins, but took my body and my soul under His protective wings. The way I mistreated myself, what someone had stolen from me, all of that was forgiven and restored to me. I only belong to God, my Father.

I came face to face with God's love and power when I was at my worst, not my best. I wasn't happy. I wasn't fulfilled. I was empty, broken, and on my knees, crying out the most ineloquent prayer in deep hopelessness and agony—in the perfect position to meet Jesus.

LOST AND WAITING TO BE FOUND

"Then cometh he to a city of Samaria...Now Jacob's well was there. Jesus therefore, being wearied with his journey, sat thus on the well...[and] there cometh a woman of Samaria to draw water." (John 4: 5–7)

IT'S HARD TO BELIEVE WHEN YOU HAVE DRAGGED YOURSELF UP TO THE world's well every day for years that God is looking out for your best interest. Sometimes it may feel like He is hidden from us or that He is choosing to remain silent. I often wondered *why* Christ was at the well in the first place? Why did He send His disciples off to town and opt to stay behind? Was He waiting for this woman so He could speak to her one on one? Certainly she had a significant purpose in God's Kingdom because she was the first to whom Jesus revealed Himself as the Messiah. As I read this story I feel Jesus obviously loved this outsider a great deal and saw potential in her. This Samaritan woman is a perfect example that right in the middle of our mess Jesus Christ is searching for us. Like the parables of the Lost Coin, Lost Sheep and Lost Son, we have a Father in Heaven who is actively seeking us out, not because *we* are good, but because He is good. We only need to let ourselves be found by Him.

I left for the military and a hopeful new start in October 2005. Out of all places for the military to send me, they moved me to Las

Vegas, a drunk-former-stripper's paradise! I met my husband, Alex, the day I moved to Las Vegas. I was walking back to my apartment complex, which he also lived in, and he hollered at me to get my attention. I want to tell you it was love at first sight, but it wasn't.

I hit the party scene really hard in Vegas. I started club hopping and becoming such a regular at places like Coyote Ugly that I soon was having VIP treatment and dancing with the girls on the bar. I got a chance to party with Paris Hilton for her birthday at Caesar's Palace, and I have been kicked out of at least three bars on the Las Vegas Strip. Not an easy feat for anyone, but I managed to do it. Three times. I was really living it up. I may not have been stripping anymore, but I still treated men the exact same way. I used them, married and single. I went on several failed dates, the last one being the absolute worst date I have ever been on. Ever. He sat across from me at Denny's flexing in a shirt he clearly got from Baby Gap and asking if his muscles looked big. I needed a steady and reliable guy. Exit Baby Gap and enter my future husband. By the way, my husband says he owes that guy a handshake. If it weren't for that terrible date, I probably would have never realized how amazing my husband is!

One afternoon I put on a tiny skirt, tank top, and high heels and decided to surprise Alex. He came to the door, shirtless, in a beanie and a pair of old jeans. And it didn't faze him in the slightest to see me dressed the way I was. That is what I love about my husband. He appreciates the makeup and dresses, but at the end of the day he loves me in a pair of jeans and a T-shirt. Up until then, every single guy I had been with wanted or expected something from me. Alex didn't want anything except a friendship. I had a hard time respecting and being comfortable around men as I got older, but with Alex I found myself becoming more and more comfortable and respecting the simplicity of his nature.

Alex had very little expectations from me and genuinely wanted to be my friend. Our first date ended with him holding my hair back over the toilet. I remember being absolutely flattered by the gesture.

Even drunk, I knew he was a good man. One night, after downing way too many Long Island Iced Tea's together, one of us joked about getting married. We *were* in Las Vegas—we should just do it. I'm happy to report that we didn't have an alcohol fueled, cliché Las Vegas wedding that night, but we did have one two weeks later!

We eloped on April 14, 2006.

We picked that date because it was a Friday and it was payday. He borrowed clothes from a friend and I wore a white halter top and a black mini skirt. First, we made the mistake of just showing up at a chapel and asking them to marry us. They informed us we need a marriage license first. Duh! We walked over to the courthouse, signed on the dotted line, and then, paper in hand, walked across the street to the chapel. We were asked what kind of wedding we wanted—Christian wedding? Jewish? Buddhist? Elvis?

"We can do anything you want here!"

Ironically enough, we opted for the Christian version. One hundred dollars later, just like that, we were married. We didn't tell anyone except a few friends. We moved into the first apartment we saw because it had a hot tub.

Although I realize that our dating story was very different from what many believe a healthy relationship is founded on, I can attest that Alex was and is still a good man. It was his goodness I was drawn to, and that goodness won out as we flipped our lifestyle on its head. We are a couple that loves to laugh a lot, and that humor has taken us through some very dark times.

We had almost nothing to our names. Everything we owned fit inside a van that we bought for five hundred dollars from a friend. We slept on a mattress from a pullout couch until someone took pity on us and gave us a used full-size mattress. Everything we owned we got for free or from thrift stores. We didn't have a table so we sat around a coffee table for dinner until my husband got mad and put his foot right through it one night. Our nightstands in our room were boxes I covered with towels.

We both struggled and fed off each other when it came to drinking. We were always going out. There are times I don't even remember making it home from the bar with him.

Needless to say, our marriage had its problems.

After one bad binge night, I realized I had a more serious problem than I'd thought. We were out with friends and I had one too many, as had my husband. Honestly, I don't even remember making it home. I just remember waking up in my underwear on the bathroom floor throwing up all over myself. I felt like my insides were going to come right out my mouth. My entire body ached. My head felt like it weighed a thousand pounds. And I just could not stop throwing up. I thought I was going to die. I ached so much my bones hurt. In fact, I would have welcomed death I was in so much pain. I slept for three days and hardly ate anything. It took about a week to fully recover.

After that, I started to take a major step toward sobriety. I cut back on what I was consuming and concentrated mostly on trying to be a good wife, despite the clearly visible cracks in our foundation. While I wasn't stone cold sober, I did manage to cut back quite a bit and I took that as a major accomplishment. Instead of drinking seven nights a week, I was only drinking two or three.

Even with all our martial problems, I wanted to bring a child into the world. Each month, we spent so much money on pregnancy tests that we should have bought stock in First Response. But eleven months into our marriage, I'd decided it was officially coming to a close. I actually made plans to move out and move in with a friend.

We made last effort plans to try and fix our relationship by taking a vacation. The weekend of our trip, I told Alex that I felt like I was getting sick. I remember coming home from work in the evenings and immediately falling asleep on the couch. I would sleep until noon, which was abnormal, even for me. I told him that I was having problems staying awake. Mentally, I counted the days in my head and realized I was a few days late. I told him to go get a test. He grumbled and slammed the door on the way out and came back with *one* test. A dollar store test.

I was pregnant.

That sobered me up overnight.

We canceled our trip and called our families. Quietly, I canceled my plans to move out and vowed to work on my marriage with Alex. We were bringing a baby into the world! I was adamant I would do whatever it took to make sure my child would not be raised the way I was. I left the military during my sixth month of pregnancy to become a stay-at-home mother after my son was born. It was completely out of my comfort zone and a huge lifestyle change.

I became restless quickly. I felt like I was losing my identity and what made me "me." I started becoming very depressed. Looking back on it now, I should have sought help instead of thinking it was just the hormones. I should have opened up and talked about it with a professional. Instead, I internalized it and became more withdrawn and despondent.

Because I felt I was losing my identity, I told my husband that as soon as I delivered and got back in shape, I would go back to work. I watched everything I consumed to make sure losing the baby weight would be as easy as possible.

The date of Mason's arrival, I was sitting at the computer when my water broke. My husband rushed me down to the hospital. I lay in that bed laboring for twenty-four hours before Mason became distressed and I had to have an emergency C-section. Even with all of that, as soon as I saw Mason, I was in love. But not just any love. This was a physical and visceral love. Never had I loved with such intensity a person I had only just met. In his book, *The Diabolist,* G.K. Chesterton wrote that God loves us with a "furious love." I get it. That is how I love my son. It's wild and protective. It just is.

It was like the entire world waited with baited breath to watch this little baby take his first breath in my arms. He was absolutely perfect. I counted his little fingers and toes. I commented on how big his feet were and gently rubbed my finger alongside his face. I couldn't stop looking at him. I couldn't believe I made something so adorable and precious. Every mistake and disappointment in my life melted away. Not a single thing mattered to me other than Mason.

We brought him home and I had complications with my C-section. I had to return back to the hospital to be cut open again. I slipped off the deep end emotionally after that.

Having a baby is traumatic enough, having to go through it again three weeks later was crushing to me. What was supposed to take six weeks to heal took three months. I came home from the hospital a changed person. I didn't want to touch my son. I didn't even want to be in the same room as him. I lay in bed and cried as my husband took care of most of the baby duties. I became angry. And if that wasn't enough, Mason was a colicky baby.

There were times I just screamed right alongside him. I knew I was losing it. I knew something was wrong, but everyone was telling me it was hormones and they would balance out. The guilt I felt from hating being a mother was enough to push me over the edge. I often contemplated adoption or just running away from my responsibilities, and then those thoughts would have me packing my bags for yet another guilt trip.

In January 2008, I decided I'd had enough. I fed Mason one last time and laid him in his bassinet in the living room, then I took several pills one by one, sat on the edge of the bed, and waited. I have very little recollection of what happened, which I believe to be a tender mercy from God. At some point, I called my mother, who panicked. She got a hold of my husband. He rushed me to the hospital.

I remember being in the hospital. I remember counting tiles on the ceiling. I remember people talking about the upcoming Super Bowl. I remember being told that I would have to be held for a 5150, a psychiatric hold, and I was not happy. I argued with the doctor. I panicked over not being able to be with Mason. I completely see the irony of that situation now. A suicidal mother worried about not being able to see her son? Truly, all confusion comes from Satan. I slept a lot, and worried even more. But when I walked out of the hospital I knew I had to keep going. I didn't know how I was going to do it, but I knew I needed to figure it out—fast.

If things weren't tough enough, two weeks after I was released from the hospital my husband received orders to deploy overseas to Korea for twelve months. I was trying to claw my way out of depression, and now I would have to do it alone. But I was determined.

We decided to sell most of our belongings while Mason and I moved to Florida to be closer to my family. I thought being in an area I was familiar with would help fix my problem. Instead, being so close to my family only hindered my healing. My mother agreed that I could stay with her while I figured out how to be on my own as a new mom. After two weeks, she decided that she couldn't handle it and kicked Mason and me out.

Out of sheer desperation and having nowhere else to go with my six-month-old son, I moved into my father's home. I felt like I was a teenager again. He pressured me to lose the baby weight and get a job. He hated the fact I had decided to stay at home with my son. He would often suggest to me that I should get a job, become financially independent, and hide the money from my husband just in case he cheated on me. My dad was preparing me for a divorce. I was given chores that were inspected when he got home from work. Everything I did became monitored, so I took to hiding in my bedroom with Mason just to stay out of the way. Finally, I had enough and moved into my own one-bedroom apartment.

Becoming a mother brought up many underlying issues that I was forced to confront. The years of abuse and the hedonistic lifestyle left scars that were so deep only a baby could bring it into focus. I was damaged and I was hurting. And now this damaged, hurting person had a tiny, vulnerable human being to care for. I had no idea what I was doing as a mother. Every part of the process felt strange and uncomfortable to me.

I still carry guilt that I need to surrender to God daily from the early years of Mason's life. Like my mother, I felt Mason had ruined my life. I started to blame him for the way I was feeling and the way I felt like my body never recovered. And to make matters worse, Mason looks just like my husband. There were times my mother came out of my mouth with, "You look just like your father." I was literally like the Lamanites, rehearsing and believing the traditions and words passed down from my parents (see Mosiah 10:11–17).

I was so angry, cold, and routine. If I varied from that routine I set for myself, I lost it. I found I functioned better with it and if I could control the circumstances, I could control the depression and anxiety. I had such bad anxiety that I was incapable of driving while Mason was in the car. I was scared to death of the other drivers. I would go 45mph in a 60mph zone. And if Mason cried, all hell would break loose.

The worst was the so called "mommy wars." You know—the impossible standards mothers set on other mothers? Because nothing shows more *empowerment* and *love* than taking a new mother and telling her everything she is doing is wrong and potentially harmful to her child: breastfeeding vs. formula feeding; cloth diaper vs. Pampers; homemade baby food vs. store bought food. It's all confusing and really, it's not strengthening or edifying to constantly critique other women.

I've learned that the best way to help a new mother is to offer willing arms to hold her baby while she finally eats a hot meal at a normal pace instead of shoveling it in her mouth like she's going through Basic Training.

Being a mother is tough. The real work begins after childbirth, and there isn't an epidural for that.

I didn't learn to love my role as a mother until after joining the LDS Church, and that only came with time and a lot of patience. Being a mother is tough. The real work begins after childbirth, and there isn't an epidural for that. It can be overwhelming and frustrating. It's a job that requires a lot of grit and a lot of grace, especially when you're staring down the clock of another sleepless night. It requires women that can dig down deep and push through all the gross and mess that comes with it. It requires us to be brave enough to be exactly how we are, because I am going to let you in on a little secret: even with all your imperfections, God handpicked you to be the mother of your specific children. I believe our children can be some of our greatest teachers of gospel truths.

Two years ago, Mason was diagnosed with Asperger's Syndrome, a high-functioning form of autism. Initially, my husband and I were devastated. We couldn't believe it and we worried about his future. It's a scary word, autism. It's overwhelming and there is too much of a stigma attached to the name. However, what felt like a burden then has now become the greatest blessing in my life, besides my relationship with Jesus Christ. My son's creativity, affection, kindness, and warmth for people have been the most beautiful thing to witness and be invited into. His world is a special one, and one that I sometimes take for granted. He has taught me patience and vulnerability, that it's okay to cry and to take a break, but it's not okay to give up. He has humbled me with his loving and forgiving hugs, even if I've not been Mother of the Year on that particular day. One bad day does not constitute my worth as Mason's mother.

He doesn't want or need a perfect mom. Mason just needs me. Arms that are just the right size to embrace him. It's okay to loosen up and not take life so seriously. It's perfectly natural to dance in the middle of the grocery aisle when a cool song comes on overhead. Seriously, we have danced our way through the frozen aisles many times to feign off a temper tantrum.

More importantly, my son has shown me the wonder of childlike faith versus my own childish faith when I don't feel like I get my way. May I never lose that sense of awe and wonder with even the simplest joys in life.

I learned to love my role as a mother as it was specific to me and my family, *with* my history as it is. There is no one better for my son and I believe that now. What we bring to our families is unique and exclusive. We are not raising our Relief Society president's children, but our own, and we are not called or set apart as mothers to keep up with anyone else. Ladies, let's stop chasing perfection and start our own progress. We are learning right alongside our children. We can never know what the future will hold for them, but I do believe that God does and will honor a mother who is willing to fight for her children.

I believe poet Carl Sandburg when he said, "A baby is God's opinion that life should go on." (Carl Sandburg, *Remembrance Rock*, 1948).

My son is a testament that God had some serious plans and a specific purpose for me. The most stunning and powerful reminders of the gospel is that God will often use broken and fragile people to carry out His purposes. My job wasn't done here. God needed my help to raise up not just a generation, but a specific *one*.

I will never have the stable, loving mother-at-home story from childhood, but that doesn't diminish my role as Mason's unique mother. I used to cringe at every single "mother talk" given in church, but now I have found peace with my circumstances. I may not have had a good relationship with my mother, but those feelings of motherhood did not escape or get lost on me. I have had tons of influential women in my life that have loved me, laughed with me, lovingly guided me, and accepted me—starting with my grandmother, who continues to be my biggest supporter and cheerleader.

"Can a woman forget her sucking child, that she should not have compassion on the son of her womb? Yea, they may forget, yet I will not forget thee." (Isaiah 49:15)

I grew up in a home where love was a moving target. One day you might hit it, the next you might not. It's enough to make you question the source of love to begin with, but because of Jesus Christ I have found a target that is immoveable. I can move forward with a conviction that I will always be able to find Him. His love is not a guessing game.

I used to have a slogan I thought was pretty catchy. It was, "When God shows up, He shows off." Now I know how much of a misconception that is. God is always with us, even when we don't feel like He is; that may be when He is the closest. God is always working, always chipping away at what is keeping us immobilized in our old way of thinking. I've stopped praying for God to show up and instead I am praying to wake up to the wonder and blessings that are already all around me.

My biggest example of God's unseen hand comes from a time when I was the most frustrated and worn out. Because of Mason's Asperger's, coupled with chronic ear infections as a baby, his speech was severely delayed. There was a time I thought Mason would never talk. We would use sign language to try and rectify the problem, but the months and then years ticked by with very little understandable speech coming from his mouth. Just thinking about it now brings a knot under my breastbone. It was an incredibly overwhelming time for my husband, Mason, and me. Through the years, coupled with intense speech therapy, Mason is all caught up on his speech. When I'm having a particularly rough day, I'll just sit down with Mason to have a simple conversation with him. It's a reminder that although things are tough and it may seem like there is no end in sight, there really is hope and healing in our future. The Lord's timetable never works in conjunction to ours, but it does work. And often, it won't be until afterward that we can realize those trials were exactly what we needed to learn grace, mercy, tenderness, and compassion. They were what was needed to make us more like Him.

My whole life I really believed that abusive traditions and patterns repeated themselves. That my son was doomed to repeat my history of abuse since my mother repeated her history in black and blue bruises on my skin. I always heard, "The apple doesn't fall from the tree," or "Abuse and addictions run in families." I'm here to tell you, with the help of Jesus Christ, that is absolutely not true and that is exactly how the adversary keeps us shackled to him, the father of all lies.

I am capable of being selfless and devoted to my son. Pure love doesn't and hasn't escaped me. By the grace and mercy of God I became a mother, and there has been no love sweeter or more fulfilling than that calling in my life...even when I'm tired and grumpy.

> **By the grace and mercy of God I became a mother, and there has been no love sweeter or more fulfilling than that calling in my life...even when I'm tired and grumpy.**

I'm not a perfect mother. I get angry and frustrated. Often, I doubt myself. Sometimes, I get the overwhelming urge to take an extended vacation. Yes, perfect may not be the word I would use to describe myself when it comes to my mothering, but I am Mason's mother and that has made my life perfect.

A few years ago, Mason and I were sitting on the couch when he grabbed my hand and put it over his heart.

"Do you feel that?" he asked me. "It's filled with Momma and Daddy's love."

My love was not lost on Mason. Somehow he was able to pick through the wreckage of my life and find that treasure deep within me; Mason brought out what was good in me. *That* has been my greatest tender mercy.

COLLIDING WITH CHRIST: THE RIGHT PLACE AT THE RIGHT TIME

4

"There cometh a woman of Samaria to draw water: Jesus saith unto her, Give me to drink…Then saith the woman of Samaria unto him, How is it thou, being a Jew, askest drink of me, which am a woman of Samaria? for the Jews have no dealing with the Samaritans." (John 4:7–9)

I LOVE THIS EXCHANGE BETWEEN THE SAVIOR AND THE SAMARITAN woman. First, Christ breaks all religious, societal, and gender rules by engaging this woman in conversation. It was unlike anything of its time and people have struggled to successfully mimic it ever since. It's hard to see past the stereotypes of people who don't look or act like us. God made man in His own image and we have returned the favor by rejecting those not necessarily made in our own image. Thankfully, Jesus Christ sees beyond the label. I loved this quote from the April 2016 general conference, *"God sees people not only as they currently are but also as they may become," Elder Kevin R. Duncan (Ensign, April 2016)*

Regardless of how we may feel about someone or how uncomfortable he or she may make us, Jesus Christ has a plan for that person and He will make that plan known, even if He has to go

43

all the way through Samaria to do it. No one is beyond the grace and mercy of God, even if their circumstances may dictate otherwise. This Samaritan woman had what it took to convince an entire town of the divinity of Jesus Christ. Jesus knew it; it's us that needs convincing.

Second, I wonder how many years this woman had walked those dusty, hot roads to Jacob's well. How tired she must have been. With her five marriages and lack of community support, how lonely, betrayed, and humiliated she must have felt to walk those streets so obviously alone. Did she feel like a failure? Was she angry? Was she bitter? Was she despondent? I believe that when we fully collide with Jesus Christ, we are beyond ready. We have hit that proverbial wall and we are done. There are times we may meet Jesus in passing and never understand who we just walked by. And then there are times when we are willing to let it all go. We are tired with the way we are living. We are worn out from the journey. We are thirsty for something more, something better. And it's at those moments that Jesus comes through our Samaria.

After my husband deployed and I moved to Florida, I decided I would start to work through all the rust my life had collected. I started playing with the idea of going to church. I tried attending a mega church, which a person could easily feel lost in. The worship services were more like rock concerts and the preacher was often energetic and inspiring, but it was hard to connect with anyone. I also tried my hand at some off-shoot churches that met in living rooms and parks, which was more like a bible study or social hour. I made friends at each place, but it did little to help me spiritually or emotionally. In fact, in some ways it made me feel even more lost and lonely, and definitely more confused. I felt extremely uncomfortable with the Christian lingo where God seemed like a Cosmic Good Buddy. The "if you can pray it, then you can make it" personalities of the mega churches didn't work with me when I struggled to even believe God could love, listen to, or use someone like me.

I wish I could write and say that I was slowly improving and that my efforts were being blessed, but I was at a standstill. I was still as angry as ever and I knew I was slipping into my old patterns of destructive thinking and behavior. Additionally, with my husband deployed to Korea, he was drinking a lot more so our marriage was really on the rocks. I spent a lot of my Friday nights waiting for phone calls that would never come because he was too drunk to dial the phone.

There was a knock on my car window, and sure enough, it was the Mormon missionaries.

I met my first set of missionaries from The Church of Jesus Christ of Latter-day Saints in August of 2008. I had been on my own for four months and I was really struggling with deployment and my baby. I had been driving back from Walmart one afternoon and Mason was screaming in the backseat. To be completely honest, I was screaming with him. I was also crying.

I had no idea what to do and my anxiety was peaking. I pulled up to my apartment complex and just sat in the car, crying. There was a knock on my car window, and sure enough, it was the Mormon missionaries. I rolled down the window and basically told them to get lost with a few choice words. I wasn't interested and now was definitely not a good time. I was rude.

They couldn't have been kinder to me. They reassured me that they didn't want to evangelize, they only wanted to help me—which they did. They helped me with my groceries and Mason. I learned they lived in my apartment complex, and soon they were coming by on their bikes to check in and see how I was doing. At one point, my apartment was broken into and the missionaries started to come by to check on my safety! Absolutely unbelievable!

I couldn't help but be curious, so when they invited me to church in October, I said sure. I laughed and told the missionaries that as soon as I walked into the church, everyone would run out screaming.

45

They assured me that would never happen. This may sound like a common theme among new converts, but I struggled with finding something to wear for church my first Sunday. I owned a dress, just not an appropriate one. I believe I opted for a pair of jeans and a nice shirt.

In the end it didn't matter, since the first weekend I went was general conference and I was literally the only person in the chapel besides these missionaries. The joke was completely on me. Sure, no one ran out screaming because *no one* showed up! What kind of church was this? I was so weirded out I ended my conversations with them, but I never forgot their kindness and compassion. And, truthfully, I was curious about the LDS faith.

I continued to pop in on different denominations throughout the months, but in secret I would research The Church of Jesus Christ of Latter-day Saints. I watched every single Mormon Message video that was available and read everything I could from the Church's website. I even went out and purchased "The Work and the Glory" video series because I mistakenly thought it was history.

I made the mistake of mentioning to family and friends that I was researching the Church and they gave me an earful of anti-Mormon literature. The number one thing I heard was it was a cult. And after being told that, I believed it. But there was a pull toward it that I couldn't deny. People claimed it was a cult, but everything I read and saw about the Church signified the opposite. My husband was one hundred percent against the Church. He saw "no drinking" and "no smoking" and refused to be part of it, even threatening me with divorce.

In March of 2009, against everyone's opinions, I decided to take the missionary lessons. I googled the nearest church, and in a tank top, a pair of shorts, and flip-flops, I drove down to the building and asked to speak to the missionaries. Unfortunately, I had the wrong ward building, but the bishop was wonderful and pointed me in the right direction. I started meeting with the missionaries regularly in my home and I loved it. I loved learning about the Church and meeting the Saints, but I hated that I couldn't tell anyone else about this newfound joy. I remember sitting in Sacrament meeting and thinking, "Holy Crap! I'm surrounded by Mormons!"

It was a huge lifestyle adjustment. Truth be told, a lot of the hobbies, music, and movies the members of the Church participated in I found to be corny, but I loved the sweet nature of it all. It was odd to attend a party that was an alcohol and drug free zone. I didn't think that even existed! It was a breath of fresh air in my world.

I told my husband about the missionary lessons, of course, but he was against them and rarely wanted to hear about them. I started to love going to church. I felt like I finally belonged in a community. For the first time ever, I was around women who actually enjoyed being mothers. They played and held my son like he was one of their own. It was very overwhelming and many times I would drive away from church in tears, not because I was sad, but because I finally felt happiness. I felt loved and wanted. I felt complete and like I had finally found a home.

I held my past close to my chest though. I rarely spoke of my life before meeting the missionaries. I was terrified of being judged among these people that represented a life that was so different than mine. I was terrified my instability would scare them off.

I will tell you there were certain things I struggled with in the beginning. For instance, I had a testimony of the Doctrines and Covenants long before I had a testimony of the Book of Mormon. Strange, huh? In fact, at my interview for baptism with my bishop when I was asked about my testimony of it, I had to answer honestly that I didn't, but I was working on it. It sufficed because I eventually was baptized. It would take an additional four years to gain a testimony of that sacred book. I'm a hard nut to crack.

I also struggled with the concept of a premortal life and that I was personally selected for the life I would have here on earth. I really fought that doctrine. I kept telling the missionaries that if given the choice I would *never* have picked the life I have been given.

Now, I can understand and appreciate—dare I even say I am grateful for?—the life I raised my hand high in the air for in the preexistence. My experiences have taught me something reading every theology book would have never been able to do—God loves me tenderly and stubbornly. And He also really likes me.

Before I was baptized, my missionaries took me to the Orlando Florida Temple for a tour. I remember thinking that it was absolutely the most beautiful building I had ever seen. Everyone that walked the grounds treated it with such reverence and awe that I remember thinking I wanted something that beautiful inside my life. Everything up until that point was chaotic and complicated. I wanted something simple. Something drenched in love. Everything I struggled to understand or gain a testimony of I realized would resolve itself in time. The basics were there. I didn't just need to be a Latter-day Saint, I wanted to be. I craved it. I desired to be baptized and so I set the date.

The entire week prior to my baptism Satan worked hard on me. I doubted my decision. I wrestled with my life and what I would be giving up. Most of my friends drank and thought Mormons were a cult. I knew dynamics would change. And then there was my husband—what would it mean for our relationship? Alex tried to be supportive when he learned I wanted to be baptized, but he couldn't get past his own feelings. He fought me, begged me, and took me on a heavy guilt trip. The night before, I decided I couldn't deal with the pressure and I would just wait until a later date to commit. But God must have been working hard on my heart all night because by the morning, I decided to do it.

"Now I say unto you, if this be the desire of your hearts, what have you against being baptized in the name of the Lord, as a witness before him that ye have entered into a covenant with him, that ye will serve him and keep his commandments, that he may pour out his Spirit more abundantly upon you?" (Mosiah 18:10)

The truth is I had nothing holding me back except fear. Fear of what people might think, fear of changing my lifestyle. But I wanted to do something for me, something that I believed would finally better me. I figured it wasn't a gang I was joining, if I didn't like it, I would bounce out. I literally thought that to myself when I drove to my baptism.

I was baptized without anyone knowing. And I mean, I told no one. Not my friends. Not my family. Not even my husband. When he called later that afternoon and I told him, he hung up on me. My tender mercy, ironically, came from a "Jack Mormon" who was drinking buddies with my husband in Korea. After I was baptized, this brother sat my husband down, patiently showed him LDS scriptures, and told him a little about the Church. Although he was no longer practicing the religion, he told Alex he believed one hundred percent in the doctrine and reassured Alex it wasn't as bad as it seemed. Fortunately, that calmed my husband's nerves and anger over my decision and softened his heart.

Even though I had no close family members or friends at my baptism, I did have several people there. It was awesome. I got a little scripture set with my name on it that I valued as a prized possession. No sooner had I got it home before my son, who was eighteen months at the time, colored all over it. I was so upset, I cried. I know it seems silly now, but at the time I was so devastated that I felt like they had been ruined. Now, I look at them as a sweet reminder of that day and how I felt toward the scriptures.

I still hold them close to my heart and see them as the Word of a Living God. I had another member of the Church give me all his old *Ensign*s—and I am talking years of *Ensign*s—as well as his old *Teachings of Presidents* manuals. I read through many of them until my husband came home from deployment and we were assigned to California. I gave them to my dad to mail to me after we had moved, but he threw them out and I never saw them again. That was heartbreaking and I still think about that when I flip through my *Teachings of Presidents* manual.

Being baptized into The Church of Jesus Christ of Latter-day Saints was not an easy decision, but I have never regretted it, even with the problems and challenges that have arisen because of it. Following Jesus has never been easy for me and I don't want anyone to think otherwise. But it has changed everything in my life. And yet, there are times I feel nothing has changed—like this is the way my life was always supposed to be. My life was supposed to have this gospel. I am supposed to know Jesus.

> **Following Jesus has never been easy for me and I don't want anyone to think otherwise. But it has changed everything in my life.**

"Behold, he changed their hearts; yea, he awakened them out of a deep sleep, and they awoke unto God. Behold, they were in the midst of darkness; nevertheless, their souls were illuminated by the light of the everlasting word; yea, they were encircled about by the bands of death, and the chains of hell, and an everlasting destruction did await them." (Alma 5:7)

I felt like I was finally waking up. I was finally prepared to hear the Word. (see Alma 32:6)

The deeper I have gotten in the gospel and the closer I have come to my Savior, the more it has brought me out of my shell. It's helped me bridge my past and my future together to make the most out of my present circumstances.

Within Christ, Amanda and Nikki converge, and somehow I have begun the process of being able to forgive myself and those around me, and move forward. But, complete disclosure, it wasn't like that in the beginning. I made a ton of mistakes. I had to learn and I had to grow. It required a lot of setbacks and failures. Unfortunately, that process is always painful and uncomfortable. Change is never easy. Uprooting ourselves and altering our lives is difficult, because even if our habits and behaviors are self-destructive, we get used to them.

It reminds me of Laman and Lemuel when they left Jerusalem. After leaving the comforts of home and venturing into the wilderness, instead of trusting in God and the promises that He made to them, they continued to look backward because they felt the promises were too far off. They were stuck on the "if only" complaint that we are so familiar with today—if only we had stayed in Jerusalem and had our riches. If only so-and-so didn't act a certain way. If only this happened, then this would be easier and I could be happy. Looking back is giving in to vain imaginations. God wants us to move forward to something better. I have learned that "if only" complaints stunted my growth with God.

Here's the thing, as we travel our path, if we don't have the support that reminds us of who we are and the potential we have as sons and daughters of God and the blessing that will come when we live in that identity, we will want to return to what we knew before.

The first thing Lehi and Nephi did for their doubting family was remind them of those blessings that were waiting for them. I'm convinced that if we are successful in the journey, it's because we have been reminded of those simple things—that we are loved, cherished, and wanted within the Body of Christ, within the Church. Wherever you are today, I would encourage you to stop at Jacob's well and let Jesus Christ reveal to you one more time that He is the Way, the Truth and the Light. Drink deeply from the well of living water before you set one more foot back on the dusty roads. Let God love you today.

5

SOFTENING HEARTS THROUGH YOUR TRANSFORMATION

"The woman then left her waterpot, and went her way into the city, and saith to the men, Come, see a man, which told me all things that ever I did: is not this the Christ? Then they went out of the city, and came unto him." (John 4:28–30)

I'T'S AMAZING THAT IMMEDIATELY AFTER THE WOMAN AT THE WELL HAD learned the identity of her Lord and Savior, she dropped her bucket and went to tell everyone she knew. She had no seminary training or Young Woman's medallion. She had never served a mission. She had one afternoon with Jesus and she was absolutely convinced. She just dropped that bucket and went to go tell everyone who would listen that the Messiah had come! It's as courageous as it is shocking, because let's face it, her status didn't change. Because she had an interaction with Jesus, she wasn't suddenly married to her now live-in boyfriend. But she was a woman transformed by Christ and for that moment, that was enough.

I think a lot of times we feel like we need to have it all together before we can ever share the gospel with the people around us. We believe that we need to live our convictions with one hundred percent accuracy before anyone will take us seriously, but that is simply not the case. Information is easy to ignore and dismiss. However, a life that has been transformed is not. Often the best missionary tool we have isn't books and pamphlets on our theology, but our heart that is rooted in God and lived out in our day-to-day lives.

For my husband and me, sitting down for an hour with the missionaries isn't what brought us to Christ. It was observing the daily interactions of faithful and devoted Latter-day Saints. Not once did we ever expect perfection, but we did expect honesty. When we were able to experience that authentic living from LDS members for ourselves, we were convinced that we were in the right place.

Sometimes, I can be really pushy. Once I converted, I want people to see Jesus the way I see Him. I want people to know Him as a Savior, not a Judge. I want people to know the joy and peace that flow from that living water. I want people to not just *know* the Book of Mormon, but love it. I want the scriptures to come alive to them. I want people to live out that freedom found in Christ. But more often than not, I'm convinced to reign my enthusiasm back a little bit, but I want it nonetheless. Why? Because that's what happens when you are changed by God. That's what happens when you feel the song of redeeming love: whether or not you have a stellar voice, you've got to sing it out.

My husband is from Reno, Nevada. His parents are divorced and remarried and, although Alex didn't journey down the exact same road as me, we share a lot in common. Alex was a frequent drug user, arrested three times and entered into a rehab facility before he even graduated high school. By the time I met him he had one DUI already.

> **For my husband and me, sitting down for an hour with the missionaries isn't what brought us to Christ. It was observing the daily interactions of faithful and devoted Latter-day Saints.**

My husband also had a gambling problem. Often in the beginning of our marriage, I would check the back account and see hundreds of dollars spent at the casinos. We both struggled with pornography in those early days.

We were always threatening each other with divorce. We fought like children because that is exactly what we were—headstrong and immature children. I wanted my husband to change, but I was unwilling to change. I wanted the freedom to do whatever I wanted, but I wanted to keep him on a tight leash. How insane is that?

It drove me crazy that he watched pornography. I would catch him all the time on the computer at 3 a.m. and find magazines all over the house. It was devastating. I felt like I was sharing my marriage with a mirage, but the irony of that situation is that I modeled the exact same pornography he was looking at. It was a sobering moment to say the least.

Along with temporarily giving up alcohol when I became pregnant, I also decided I would stop watching pornography. This might sound strange, but I thought me watching it would somehow filter down to my son who was growing in my womb. Breaking free from that addiction was not easy because it is so accessible and accepted.

It was hard to leave behind because I could view pornography and then I could hide it. Pornography is dangerous because it affects the heart—the place where the Holy Ghost calls home. We have these God-given desires within us, but when we view pornography, those desires get distorted and we lose our ability to trace those desires back to the source—God. It changes your perception on love and relationships and it takes something so intimate and exploits it. It places demands and expectations on a relationship that no human being can ever live up to. I learned the hard way that everything within the business is an over-exaggerated lie. And marriage isn't like that. It's real, and there are real people's emotions and well-being attached to every action and every decision that we make. We can either hurt each other or we can edify each other. The choices are ours—and only ours—to make.

Marriage really strips away the illusion of sex that is drilled into us daily through TV, movies, and other media outlet. When the honeymoon period is over, marriage can be…well, kind of boring and predictable. Most of us live with ordinary people with ordinary functions that we can't Photoshop for our pleasure. We live with people with bad breath, body odors, thinning hair and excess belly fat that wasn't there a few years ago. We get tired, frustrated and moody. We live with people who require compassion, charity, understanding, and an endless amount of forgiveness and tolerance. And the pendulum swings both ways.

Is it any wonder that Christ calls himself "the Bridegroom" and the Church "His Bride"? It's a love that honors fidelity, a love that willingly hangs on against all the odds and fights it out. People change and so do marriages, but the covenants will always remain the same.

I used to be so envious of those husbands that bore their testimony in church and spoke about their wives lovingly over the pulpit. Later, I realized that even those marriages had their fair share of problems too. Relationships become stronger when they are pushed to the point of breaking and still do not break. Like us, our relationships will also be put through a fire and become refined as we journey through this life. They will come out purified and holy. We put our shoulder to the wheel in our marriages the exact same way we do in church and in our parenting—what we are participating in has eternal significance and it's worth our time and attention.

There are so many people struggling with pornography and want so desperately to let that sin fall away. We may feel embarrassed to talk about it, and therefore we hinder the process to heal. Open confession silences the shaming voices inside our heads. We are only as sick as our secrets. When we openly confess them, our secrets no longer control us. There are people in place, such as your bishop, that are there to help you, but if you are looking for a permanent fix, only Jesus can do that and make it last.

I found Helaman 5:10 to be an incredible source of comfort for me. It says,

"The Lord surely should come to redeem his people, but that he should not come to redeem them in their sins, but to redeem them from their sins."

Christ came to save us *from* our sins, and we need Him. We can't save ourselves. There is nothing you have done or will do on your way to the Celestial Kingdom that can't be redeemed. But I want to make perfectly clear that what we go through to commit sin distances us from our Father in Heaven. Something deep inside of us changes through the very act of our willful disobedience and there is no guarantee we will ever come back to Him. Blocking the adult websites, putting parental controls on the TV, and throwing out the smart phone can seem too radical, but they are not radical enough. You have to be radically willing to let go of your old habits and behavior. It will take a radical change of heart and a willingness to surrender to God to allow Jesus to save you from that sin.

"And now, my sons, remember, remember that it is upon the rock of our Redeemer, who is Christ, the Son of God, that ye must build your foundation; that when the devil shall send forth his mighty winds, yea, his shafts in the whirlwind, yea, when all his hail and his mighty storm shall beat upon you, it shall have no power over you to drag you down to the gulf of misery and endless wo, because of the rock upon which ye are built, which is a sure foundation, a foundation whereon if men build they cannot fall." (Helaman 5:12)

God, knowing us better than we know ourselves, is hardly surprised when we fail and take a few steps backward. The moment we are most aware of our inadequacies is when we are probably the closest to God. God is close to those with broken hearts and contrite spirits *(see 2 Nephi 2:7)*, and what's more broken and humbling than a person that admits they can't do it on their own? But the thing that we need to remember is that we need to *keep returning* to that solid foundation over and over again.

"The devil... shall have no power over you." (Helaman 5:12)

Pornography only has power if you let it have power over you. Because we have Christ on our side, we have more power than we give ourselves credit for. Through Him, we can have victory over the adversary.

What if the urge to view pornography returns?

"And it came to pass that the Lamanites said unto him: What shall we do, that this cloud of darkness may be removed from overshadowing us?... You must repent, and cry unto the voice, even until ye shall have faith in Christ... and when ye shall do this, the cloud of darkness shall be removed from overshadowing you." (Helaman 5:40–41)

You must cry out to Heavenly Father and *keep* crying out until the urge passes. There is no time limit with God, so cry out as long as you need to. I've been on my knees for unbelievably long periods of time, and every time I have risen victorious. But it's not a once-in-a-while thing, it's a constant yielding of my own will aligning it with His. One of the fruits of the Spirit is self-control, which means that it doesn't come naturally to us. We must work on it with Him who works on us. All things are possible with God. Remember, the power of Christ endows us with the power to change.

My last bit of encouragement to those who are struggling and have slid back:

"And it came to pass that they were overshadowed with a cloud of darkness, and an awful solemn fear came upon them. And it came to pass that there came a voice as if it were above the cloud of darkness, saying: Repent ye." (Helaman 5:28–29)

No matter how far into the darkness you have traveled, God still calls after you.

I do have some advice for spouses that are caught in the middle of loving their spouse and dealing with their spouse's addiction to pornography: It is not your fault. You have done nothing wrong. You are not lacking as a spouse, as a woman/man, or as a child of God. Where is God while you are hurting? I promise you, God is in the person that hurts, not in the person that does the hurting.

Finding forgiveness and rebuilding trust within our marriage was only possible when we added a third party—Christ. Like an arm that has been broken, it takes time to heal, but it will heal and eventually serve up to its full potential.

Because God has given His children their agency, we cannot force or give ultimatums to our spouses to change. But we can be firm. I learned to set firm boundaries with my husband. I told him the consequences if his actions continued, then bravely stood aside and let him make his decision and let the pieces fall where they may.

Finding forgiveness and rebuilding trust within our marriage was only possible when we added a third party—Christ.

When someone is struggling, blaming is not the solution. Brow beating them with our testimonies is counterproductive. When we speak God's truth, we are speaking with the breath of God, but when we speak out of turn and without the Spirit, it's just bad breath. This is how we make enemies instead of converts. The most important thing we can do is find those shame-free parts of the heart where God's love can still be heard, received, and embraced by those who believe they are too far gone. It reminds me of Laman and Lemuel in the Book of Mormon. In 1 Nephi 2, Lehi speaks a promised blessing over the brothers. God, as well as Lehi, obviously saw a lot of potential in Laman and Lemuel. The problem was Laman and Lemuel didn't see it in themselves and because of that they spiraled downward and began a generation filled with hate and revenge.

As someone who did a lot of yelling to my husband about what pornography was doing in my marriage, I now realize I was drowning out the Spirit to speak comforting words to me and through me. No amount of pleading or threatening my husband could change what only God could do. When a spouse is addicted to pornography, there is a disconnect with your spouse and it's a wire that only God can reconnect.

Staying close to the Savior and allowing Him to carry me is one of the only ways I was able to make it through that season of my life, and pretty much every season to follow. Choosing to follow Him while the world around me seemed to fall apart only served to strengthen my relationship with Jesus. A relationship that has never disappointed or hurt me. When my relationship with Jesus is right, all other relationships fall into place.

I turned my priority from my husband to my God and, because of that, God could work on my husband's heart. I was standing in the way too much. God met me within my breaking and showed me that, despite it all, I am loved fully and completely and that worth is not dictated by what my spouse does or doesn't do. And in a true twist of irony that only God could provide, I was able to heal from my own sordid past with pornography. God truly uses trials and suffering to help us grow; if nothing else, it teaches us how to show mercy and grace to those who are hurting us.

I wish I could write solid advice on how to get your spouse to stop viewing pornography, but I can't. However, having ridden both sides of the fence, I can tell you that while pornography will damage a relationship, it doesn't have to break it. As an addict, it hardened my heart to receive love, and as a spouse of an addict, it made me feel exposed and betrayed. Only love has the power to disarm a person and promote change. It isn't easy. But it is the way of the disciple. Love will always win.

Alex, realizing that he no longer wanted to pollute our marriage with harmful toxins, set out to learn more about the Church for himself. I was baptized in June 2009 and attended church alone with Mason for a couple months while Alex sat on the sidelines and observed. He saw the changes that I was making and the joy I was finding as a new convert and naturally, he got curious. We invited the missionaries over in October of that year for him to begin taking the lessons with them. I don't remember the details, but I do remember my husband saying over and over, "I just feel so good when they are around. I like them here." It's a testament that is shared by many new converts as the missionaries bring the sweet and tender spirit of the Lord with them.

He watched as my ward family rallied around Mason and me. He witnessed love and affection poured out on us. He heard my joy, observed my growth, and God broke through that wall of his and spilled over into his life almost unannounced. No one said or did anything extraordinary, but they loved his family and that was enough. I think that is what I love the most about the Church. When you sit back and look at it as a whole, it's just ordinary individuals doing the extraordinary. It truly has the power of God as the undercurrent in the ocean of the Saints. It's almost tangible and it's what brought my husband into the waters of baptism in December 2009.

If you get anything from this book, I pray you understand these two things: Anyone at anytime can start a new future because of Jesus Christ and His Atonement. And there is nothing that you have done or will ever do that can't be used to bring God glory and further His Kingdom. Sometimes what we feel are our biggest failures may be the one thing God is using to bring you to Him. If we have an encounter with Jesus, it's because He has been orchestrating it from the very beginning. All we have to do is wake up. It is the simple love and gestures that testify the most powerfully to an individual looking for living water. We can shout the gospel with our lives when we love without borders, judgment, or fear. All we need to do is share the gospel and allow God the room to do what He does best—bringing the dead back to life.

I entered into my marriage recklessly on a cool spring night in Las Vegas and firmly believed the misconception that love, like a romantic movie, would definitely keep us together. "Love is all you need," sang The Beatles, but I disagree. What you need is grit, perseverance, humor, and God. I now walk with a steady step in my marriage knowing that even with all of its broken parts, disappointments, and struggles, my marriage has shown me what it truly means to be in love.

Marriage is not only a calling; it is an honor.

WHEN MY IDOLS CRASHED DOWN

"Jesus saith unto her, Woman, believe me, the hour cometh, when ye shall neither in this mountain, nor yet in Jerusalem, worship the Father. Ye worship ye know not what." (John 4:21–22)

HOW OFTEN DO WE GET CAUGHT UP IN WORSHIPPING OUR MAN-made gods? We think we have the "right" god because it gives us a small amount of pleasure, whether that be through popularity, wealth, or respect. But is it really the Holy and True God?

Sometimes, I think we get so wrapped up in worshipping the culture of God instead of the Creator. We think we have to perform to gain God's approval, but what God says is that, "You already have my approval because of my Son, Jesus Christ. Stop giving me a show and give me your heart."

Following Jesus takes work, and, admittedly, during my first couple years in the church, I wasn't willing to put forth the work. I am the first to confess that initially I was baptized for the people. I fell in love with the Saints. They were nurturing and loving toward me when I needed it the most. I felt special and for the first time, I felt worthy. Sadly, very little of those feelings equated to Jesus and knowing that He feels the exact same way about me.

Unfortunately, the honeymoon period of my baptism wore off. Suddenly, what made me special at my baptism made me different every Sunday after that. I could feel the divide between me and everyone else. It felt so tangible and so real, like a wall that I couldn't get over no matter how hard I tried. And I definitely did try.

Adult Children of Alcoholics, an organization that works with adults who were raised in alcoholic families, has something called The Laundry List—14 Traits of an Adult Child of an Alcoholic (see www.adultchildren.org/lit-Laundry_List for more information). Some of the traits are,

1. We become isolated and afraid of people and authority figures.

2. We become approval seekers and lose our identity in the process.

3. We get feelings of guilt when we stand up for ourselves instead of giving in to others.

4. We are dependent personalities who are terrified of abandonment and will do anything to hold on to a relationship in order not to experience painful abandonment feelings, which we have received from living with sick people who were never there emotionally for us.

In a nutshell: we don't talk, don't trust, don't feel. We just do.

I approached my initial walk within the Church and with Jesus the exact same way. I imagined Christ's eyes rolling as I found my way back under the cross again for yet another failure or mistake. I could almost hear Him whisper, "Oh no, not you again." I saw my Heavenly Father as stern, cold, and harsh like my own father, always quick to point out my flaws and never eager to extend a loving hand without a lecture.

I really tried hard to embrace that homemaking culture everyone seems to love so much. I tried my hand at sewing, baking, canning, gardening, crocheting, and scrapbooking. Each hobby ended in frustration and tears. I am just not that woman. The more I tried to mold myself after the image of other Latter-day Saint women, the more disenchanted I became with the Church.

I started growing angry, cynical, and judgmental. The more I tried and my efforts were ignored or overlooked, the more I began to rethink my decision to be with the Latter-day Saints. Because I didn't feel like I fit in, it affected how I thought God looked at me. "We approve of this behavior, Nikki, therefore this is the behavior that best satisfies God." I came to see my Father in Heaven as a man sitting in a Lazy Boy, demanding a sandwich with some homemade jelly on it.

I tried to adjust. But the more I tried to adjust, the more I felt uncomfortable with myself, like I was neglecting certain attributes and talents that God had given me. I felt as if I was becoming a woman I didn't know, and if I were to be completely honest, I didn't like. Yes, I fully acknowledged that there were behaviors I needed to change that were not conducive to a God-saturated life, but my personality? I felt like I needed to edit my life if I ever wanted to fit in. It's extremely discouraging to be asked to separate yourself from the journey that led you to Jesus Christ. If you're not familiar with the nature of Christ, it can be so easy to mistake His nature for that of the culture. If you feel rejected by the culture, you can feel rejected from the Savior.

My struggles weren't just isolated with me, but my husband also experienced his own challenges. He had a hard time relating to the Priesthood, which was worlds away from the life that he grew up in. Often, he'd complain that all anyone did was talk about where they were succeeding, when he longed to hear, "I'm struggling with..." It's easy to feel like you fall short when you compare yourself to the success of others.

To make matters worse, all of our friends walked away from us when they learned we were Mormon. I'm not kidding—no one wanted to hang out with people who didn't drink anymore. All we had was each other, and we started driving each other crazy. Alex really wrestled with that. He often threatened to leave me so he could be with his friends again. Everyone seemed to be having a great time without us. Granted, all of our friends are divorced now, but at the time all we understood was the overwhelming loneliness. Over time, it just didn't seem worth it anymore. We were ready to throw in the towel.

Prior to joining the Church, I really worked hard at conforming to the standards my family and friends put on me. I needed to be thin, blonde, the life of the party, sexy at all times, always available, never emotional, and always down for a good time. When I joined the Church, I felt the exact same pressure to conform to the standards that other Church members felt the need to place on me, i.e., you must love being a homemaker and all things crafty, never watch anything other than PG movies, get rid of all your clothing, have more children, and never ever let on that all of this makes you extremely uncomfortable. The first year after my baptism, my husband bought me a sewing machine, which was only used once at a Relief Society activity where I clumsily and awkwardly tried to thread the needle. I have a shelf filled with books on how to sew and crochet that have collected layers of dust.

I have thrown more crochet needles across the room in frustration than anyone else I know. My first attempt at making a blanket turned into a giant dreadlock braid because I couldn't figure out how to hook the yarn to start another row. I tried to bake, but I almost burned my house down. Over the years, my sweet and ever patient husband would allow me the freedom to "find my way," but always dropped reminders that, "Anytime you want to go back to being Nikki, I'll be waiting."

Recently, I did learn how to can and my husband treated it like I just told him I was pregnant. At first he was shocked, then he cried tears of joy, and then he was over the moon excited as he talked about it for days and days afterward.

I had a bishop say to me one time after I lamented I was a terrible Latter-day Saint woman, "Nikki, all that stuff is great—gardening, sewing, canning—but none of it will ever get you into Heaven." He was absolutely right. There is a huge difference between suffering to the end and enduring to the end, and what I was doing was borderline torturous to me.

Looking back, I realize how wrong I had been in reconstructing myself in the beginning of my membership. I was living as an imposter. I was too worried about pleasing people instead of pleasing my Father in Heaven. I was banking on mercy from my

> **"Nikki, all that stuff is great—gardening, sewing, canning—but none of it will ever get you into Heaven."**

fellow Saints, instead of relying completely on the mercy from Him who came for me while I was still a sinner and not only loves me, but is fond of me. I feared my community's opinions and their judgments. I hid what made me special and opted to live one foot out the door in my relationship with God because I refused to live honestly and authentically. God didn't want to work with a wholly different person—God chose me, even with all of my baggage. God made me knowing I would never enjoy sewing or be a soft-spoken Latter-day Saint woman, and He seems to be perfectly content with that, so maybe I should be too.

When God looked over all that He created He said that it was good, and nothing will ever change that truth, whether you look like your neighbor or not. In the world to come, I will not be asked, "Why weren't you like your Relief Society president?" I will be asked why was I not Nikki Yaste, the flawed but irreplaceable person in whom God has sent his Spirit to dwell.

There has never been and there will never be another person just like you. You are the direct evidence of the love of God, who has personally invested Himself in you. We do not need to cheapen that by trying to mimic our neighbors, no matter how lovely or incredibly talented they may be. When we worship in unity, not uniformity, that's where we will have the biggest impact on the community around us. Only when we share the same vision and the same eternal goal without sacrificing the divine gifts and talents God has individually given us will we better be able to serve one another within the church.

I try to remember that bishop's advice when I feel the pressure to fit in with women that have different hobbies than me. We are all unique and special and I have learned to love each and every gift a Latter-day Saint woman brings to God's table. And I really appreciate them for allowing me to raid their fantastic gardens, because mine just keeps dying on me.

Fear and rejection are counterproductive to the Christian life. Strength comes from knowing with a bold confidence and security who I am in Christ and applying it to my own mortal journey. We all may be traveling in the same direction, but the view will always look different to each one of us. One journey will not be better than the other, but all are found walking with Jesus Christ. We are not given a spirit of fear and rejection, but of love, peace, and the courage to accept who we truly are, not who we think we should be. Truthfully, God will always be more concerned with how you are turning out despite any relationships and circumstances that you may find yourself in.

In Romans 10:11 it says, *"For the scripture saith, whosoever believeth on him shall not be ashamed."* Not feeling ashamed comes from the definite knowledge that we do not belong to this world with its tattered and broken opinions. We are called to rise above it and lock our eyes with Jesus. And surely, those feelings of "not feeling ashamed" go both ways. God is not ashamed to call you His just because you play a different part of the orchestra than the rest of us. It's all beautiful music directed by Him anyways.

Jesus came in the fullness of grace and truth, and the truth shall set you free *(see John 8:32)*. Are we living a life in freedom? Or are our worries and insecurities of what other people think of us weighing us down and crushing us underneath its feet? If it's the latter, we haven't truly embraced the goodness of the gospel. It's called the "good news" for a reason. It is a gospel that brings life, not death through fear. Listen for the Voice that calls you to come out of those fears of opinions and judgments, even your own opinion about yourself, and learn to trust the Voice that sings over us.

"The Lord thy God in the midst of thee is mighty; he will save, he will rejoice over thee with joy; he will rest in his love, he will joy over thee with singing." (Zephaniah 3:17)

Despite what people may say or think about you, you belong to God. We are important to Him. We matter deeply to the Maker of all matter. We are here because He wants us to be. *"Why shouldn't it intensify our sense of identity and self-respect and hope for the future to know that we are the spiritual offspring of God?" Elder Jeffrey R. Holland* (Holland, *Ensign,* April 1980)

The healing process begins when we learn to turn away from our idols, our need to perform and impress, and when we redirect our gaze to the face of Jesus Christ, who wants us to trust Him enough to be ourselves. I had to learn, and relearn, to see myself through the eyes of Heaven—and it will forever be an ongoing process. It's much easier to embrace my flaws and drown in self-pity. It takes determined discipline to rise above opinions, even my own.

The healing process begins when we learn to let go of our father "figures" and embrace the true Father, our Heavenly Father. What does God see when He looks at His children? He sees Christ. He doesn't see your past, your brokenness, your insecurities and failures, He sees Jesus. We are covered like a blanket by the Atonement. We had a purpose long before someone ever had an opinion. What God says about us is reality and that settles it. The rest is someone else's problem to deal with.

When the military moved us to North Dakota, we decided to leave the Church and religion altogether. We fell, rather quickly, back into our addictive behaviors.

I started modeling pornography again. We both started drinking. We started losing ourselves in other things. Alex began filling his time with work and I lived in the gym. We fought constantly over the smallest things. We basically started behaving like we had never been introduced to the gospel, but inside something had changed. Every modeling gig, every drink I took, everything felt different.

I knew I was more than this. I knew that I was living a lie on all fronts. I knew I had a home because I had found it once and this wasn't it. My life was missing its important piece, Jesus Christ.

We spent a year and a half away from Church until my husband received orders to deploy once again overseas. This time it would be different. When he left, I told him there would not be one drop of alcohol in our home under any circumstances, and proudly, that is one commitment that I have kept one hundred percent. I immediately stopped all modeling jobs and didn't return their phone calls.

But the number one thing I knew I needed to change was my attendance in church. I could change everything about myself, but I knew without a doubt that it wouldn't last unless I committed myself to going back to church and living the gospel. I was more than my past. I was more than my mistakes. I have a lot to offer and I wasn't going to allow myself to be pushed out of the arms of Jesus for one second more.

Like the prodigal son, the way I was living was going to kill me one day. I needed to be better for my son, and I longed to feel the warm embrace of the Father. But I was adamant I would be going back to church as me. Not as some carbon copy of what someone thought I should be, but as Nikki. I am tattooed, sometimes loud, really energetic, kind of sarcastic, and definitely a convert to Mormonism. I wasn't going to hide anymore because it did a lot more damage to my walk with Jesus than it helped. I was going to start speaking openly about what I was struggling with. I figured if I was struggling, chances are there were other people struggling too. I would be that sister that I wish I would have had in my life initially.

And I would love everyone openly and courageously through the stereotypes.

Instead of moving our tiny family to Florida like I had previously done when my husband deployed, we decided to move to Reno, Nevada, to get to know my husband's family. I always loved Reno. I fell in love with that city from the moment I visited it after my husband and I had eloped. I was stoked to be given the opportunity to call it home.

I googled the Church before moving and I learned that there were quite a few members living in Northern Nevada, that excited me. I called my future bishop to tell him that there was going to be a new family in the ward. I did it more out of a courtesy. Because I am heavily tattooed, I knew there would be looks and possibly some comments made. I do remember he laughed when I told him about my tattoos and said, "You can still come to church with tattoos."

Yeah, I didn't think he realized just how much I was covered and how visible my tattoos were. These were not ankle butterflies we were talking about. They were sleeves and chest pieces. I believe I laughed at him and told him something along those lines as well.

The week we moved into our home, my new bishop came and visited us. He showed up expectantly, which surprised us. He sat in the middle of our messy, unpacked living room and just chatted with us. We immediately felt at ease with him. To this day, my husband and I still talk about how special it made us feel that he took the time to do that simple and welcoming gesture for us. We have felt in the past like we were somehow "less than," especially compared to those born and raised within the church. That visit he made to us set the tone for me. He made us feel like our family was not only needed in the ward, but also like we belonged there. Like, *welcome home* and *we have been waiting for you.*

Sometimes, I wonder how differently that would have gone for us if he hadn't taken that extra step to fulfill his calling as a bishop in that capacity. We needed that visit from him first to ease our minds about coming back to church. Clearly, I believe God had His hand in that special moment. Exactly one year later, this bishop would escort my husband through the temple and be a witness at our sealing. His family has become our friends, though for me it may be a little deeper. Whether he is aware of it or not, that bishop became a kind of father to me. A burden or responsibility he didn't ask for, but I trusted him, something that doesn't come easy for me. In return, he trusted me, encouraged me, guided me, and gave me the space to spread my wings and find Jesus, not on anyone else's terms, but my own. Dare I suggest that he, somehow, saw potential in me and got me to see it in myself? He dared me to take off my spiritual makeup, stop trying to become some ideal Mormon, and start to smile at what made me, me.

In return, I became more open, affectionate, and sincere about building a relationship with Jesus Christ. Before I went to the temple I made a joke in poor taste that I *definitely* needed to change my personality now since I was going to the temple. Without missing a beat, that bishop said, "Nikki, don't you ever change a thing about you." There have been few people in my life that have dared to make that declaration, no strings attached.

Honestly, I don't know where I would be without his loving example of the priesthood. I firmly believed that priesthood correlated to machoism and I wanted nothing to do with it, especially after being mistreated by men in my life.

One time, I asked him how long he had been a bishop and his reply was something along the lines of, "Almost five years. Why? Do I still look like I don't know what I'm doing?"

I loved that because it was honest. I would be wrong to think that every single man that holds the priesthood is worthy of that honor and privilege, but this man magnified his calling in a life-changing way. Joseph Smith gave us this revelation in D&C 121: 39–40:

"We have learned by sad experience that it is the nature and disposition of almost all men, as soon as they get a little authority, as

they suppose, they will immediately begin to exercise unrighteous dominion. Hence many are called, but few are chosen."

Yes, I readily recognize that there are men that will abuse that authority, but as long as I can count on at least one hand the men that are decent, honorable, honest, and trying to do the best they can, I can sustain the priesthood. That bishop was a powerful example that there are good and decent men in the world that just want to do the right thing. Bishops have an incredible responsibility that they must shoulder on a daily basis, but I am proof that it's the simplest gestures and forms of love that make the biggest impact on a member. You don't have to move the mountain in front of me, you simply need to walk next to me or shout up encouragement. I'll get up there, eventually.

As long as I can count on at least one hand the men that are decent, honorable, honest, and trying to do the best they can, I can sustain the priesthood.

We promised our new bishop we would be at church the following Sunday. Complete disclosure, I was very nervous—I felt sick to my stomach getting ready for church. I came very close to pulling the plug, and if it weren't for the promise we made to the bishop, I probably would have asked to turn the car around. For kicks, I wore a spaghetti strap dress because I had it in my head that I would just shock people and then pull back the reins—Here are all my tattoos! Let's just move on together!

People could not have been more open and loving toward us.

We were immediately invited over to homes for dinners, and we had a steady stream of visitors, like Ron and Annette Perry, who would become like adoptive parents to me. That LDS family that I really coveted as a new believer was fulfilled in this ward.

We walked out that first Sunday, not only filled with the Spirit, something that had been void in our lives for the last year and a half, but filled to the brim knowing that God had led us to good people. For the first time since my husband had joined the military, he felt safe leaving Mason and me behind for a deployment because he knew we were in capable hands with our new ward family. We would be ok. See, here's the beautiful part about the gospel: though our friends had abandoned us and our families didn't agree with our faith, it was okay. Because of the gospel, we traded out our earthly families for an eternal one. The fellowship runs deep within the LDS community. We would be okay.

I didn't get a huge "welcome home" banner when I arrived at my new ward and I certainly didn't get a party, though Scriptures tell us that *"there is joy in the presence of the angels of God over one sinner that repenteth,"* (Luke 15:10) so maybe there *was* a party! I did, however, get something better. I got to know Jesus in that ward. Often, God's love will only be perceived through human flesh, especially when a person is hurting and damaged, which I was. I felt God's love through the ordinary human beings attending in the Pyramid Lake Ward in Sparks, Nevada, and I experienced the mission of the Church—my head belief became my heart belief.

The Perrys took me under their wings and called me family. They became a place of refuge, dinners, laughter, Nicolas Cage jokes, and late-night Billy Joel music videos. They showed up to watch my son play football and hollered encouragement even when he was clearly smashed by the other team.

When my husband came home for his mid-tour they offered us a kid-free night so we could have some alone time before he returned to the desert. Annette was my escort through the temple and I felt so at ease with her. No matter how ridiculous I was, Annette just loved me. The night I went to the temple for my endowments, I fretted over the thought of wearing garments and worried that they would be uncomfortable. I told Annette that I was worried I would feel like a pot roast with a string tied around it. When I finally was able to get dressed into them, I shouted, "Yes! They fit!" Most people would have been horrified, but not Annette. She laughed and cheered with me! No matter how insane or outrageous, Annette gave me the courage to just be myself. The Perrys showed me what it was like to have a Christmas saturated in Christ, giving it real meaning and depth. And the first time I was asked to speak in Sacrament meeting, Ron texted me encouragements during it to make me smile. They were so proud. And like my bishop, Ron was also a great example of a faithful Latter-day Saint. Ron was the one who laid his hands on my husband's head to give him the Melchizedek Priesthood.

There are so many of us who feel ashamed to come home because we think what we have done is too bad and we don't want to face the music. But the music isn't funeral music—it's celebration music from a party that is being prepared for you. We don't need to have a long-winded explanation as to why we are coming home. The Father isn't standing outside the door, hands on hips, lecture on His lips. No, He waits by the window, looks over the horizon, and runs out to greet us while we are still a long way off.

Hands down one of the most beautiful verses in the Book of Mormon is when He says he must go visit the lost tribes of Israel and he says, *"for they are not lost unto the Father." (3 Nephi 17:4)*

Everyone is important. Everyone is accounted for. Our Father wants us home more than we could ever possibly want to be home.

7

WORKING THROUGH OFFENSES

"And upon this came his disciples, and marvelled that he talked with the woman: yet no man said, What seekest thou? or, Why talkest thou with her?" (John 4:27)

WHILE JESUS CHRIST IS TALKING TO THIS OUTCAST OF A WOMAN and the disciples happened to walk up mid-conversation, I always wonder how many sideway glances and awkward, forced smiles they gave this woman while they gathered around to hear the ending of their conversation. How often do we judge others simply because they fail differently than we do? Jesus asks us to look beyond the skin and see sin as something foreign to a person. It's easy to write, hard to put into practice.

People can be cruel and insensitive, myself included. I have had so many offensive remarks and behavior directed toward me, that it's getting its own chapter. I felt like because I traveled a different path, some thought it was okay to say whatever because I was "used to it" or I'd "heard it all before."

In 1 Nephi 8:21, Lehi has a vision of a *"numberless concourses of people...pressing forward that they might obtain the path which led to the tree [of life]."* Only by the grace and tender mercy of Jesus Christ, the iron rod, were they able to taste the sweet fruit that comes from knowing the Atonement of Christ. However, it says that after they partook of the fruit some were ashamed. I think a lot of times we translate that scripture to mean "the Saints" versus "the world," but when I read it, I read of a Saint who has had moral failures and is being made to feel ashamed of their sin. Every time we make someone feel like they are somehow less in the eyes of Jesus, that they do not belong by the tree of life, we have taken up residency inside the great and spacious building. I think one of my most favorite tongue-in-cheek quotes about the Saints came from Brigham Young: "To live with the Saints in Heaven is bliss and glory. To live with the Saints on Earth is another story." (Holzapfel and Holzapfel, *Women of Nauvoo*, 1992)

Boy, was he right! We are all broken vessels and yet, we can't stop awkwardly pointing out the cracks in everyone else's containers. I have had people judge me or falsely accuse me, I have been ostracized or pigeonholed, I have been called the Mormon Stripper, the Mormon Suicide Girl, the Mormon Slut, and "the type of girl that can't be trusted around the priesthood." I have had my blog linked to pornography sites. I've had Saints inquire about my old pornography pictures. I've been taken too seriously or not seriously enough. I've been looked at like a project and an object.

Basically, if there was a way to make someone feel like they are "less than," I have experienced it.

My first experience with being deeply offended came at a BBQ with some people in my ward and I was wearing a pair of shorts that, admittedly, were pretty short. I remember a conversation about the temple came up and I expressed that one day, I would love to go. A sister laughed at me and said, pointing directly at my bare legs, "You will never go dressed like that."

I was so offended by that. Mostly, I didn't know there was anything wrong with the way I dressed, I figured it was just clothing, and the amount of changing and shifting I did to become a Latter-day Saint was already great. But apparently there were other people who had some issues with my fashion choices.

An older sister—and I mean several decades older and at least two sizes bigger than me—dropped off her 1980's shoulder-pad-floral dresses in a bag on my front step and told me that I should give them a try. I threw them in the garbage on my way inside.

I have left or struggled with remaining a member of The Church of Jesus Christ of Latter-day Saints because of its people. I love the faith, please don't misunderstand me, but I have been hurt because of its members more than enough times. I have shed tears and have gotten into many (and I do mean many) arguments with my husband because of other people's actions. I always hated the saying, "The church is perfect, but the people are not." Mostly because I believe we, the people, *are* the church. The gospel is perfect. But as members, we run the risk of representing Him wrongly and diluting who He truly is. When I decided to take a break from church, it wasn't Heavenly Father or Jesus Christ I was rejecting, but His people.

"Have you noticed how easy it is to cross over the line and find fault with other people? Mercy for me, justice for everyone else is a much too common addiction." Elder Cree L. Kofford (Ensign, May 1999)

But herein lies the reality of a truth that I needed to learn: sometimes righteous people do and say unrighteous things to each other. And I need to forgive, as I would like to be forgiven, instead of demanding justice for those who made me feel bad, while begging for mercy for the times when I hurt others.

For every one person that has made me feel like I didn't belong, there has been someone else that made me feel loved and included. Sometimes I hated myself for not having supernatural vision before my conversion to see into the future. Why didn't

> **I need to forgive, as I would like to be forgiven, instead of demanding justice for those who made me feel bad, while begging for mercy for the times when I hurt others.**

an angel appear to me and stop me from acting like a fool for fun? Couldn't God clue me in on the scrutiny I'd be under as an adult? But no angel appeared to me or to anyone else who has maybe stumbled. That deserves mercy all on its own.

"The light of the body is the eye; if, therefore, thine eye be single, thy whole body shall be full of light." (3 Nephi 13:22)

Are we being critical? Judgmental? Superficial? Or are we kind and compassionate? The way we see each other is a reflection of how we see ourselves. How much we judge another person will always depend on how deeply we choose to look at a person in front of us, how much we are willing to share in their story and to understand the mileage worn on their shoes, how much we are willing to read the human behind the face. Does it really matter what someone looks like to a person who only wants to look like Jesus?

Here is a truth that you can cling to: only hurting people hurt people.

"But those things which proceed out of the mouth come forth from the heart; and they defile the man."(Matthew 15:18)

Here's the irony though, those who offended me have a lot more in common with me than we care to discuss. I, too, live with insecurities and anxiety. I wrestle with doubt in my faith and I sometimes wonder if God really does care. I struggle in my marriage and as a mother, a woman, a Saint. What is most personal to us is most universally felt by everyone, whether you are a "lifer" within the Church or a newly baptized convert.

"Spiritual wounds are not easily visible, except with inspired eyes."
President Henry B. Eyring (Ensign, May 2009)

In the past, I have believed in the eye for an eye mentality. If someone hurt me or a person I loved, I would have sought revenge. Now, I seek Jesus. I've learned to allow God into my heart to change me, to change my perspective to see that person, not as my enemy, but as a brother or sister that is hurting. The hardest, most rewarding prayer I have ever had to pray is, "My Heavenly Father, you know exactly how I feel about that person, but I am open to you changing that."

Is it eloquent? No. But it lets God know that I am the one that needs to have a change of heart first, and only He will be able to do it. Often, the primary revelation that is restored to us is that God loves everyone, even those who irritate us.

> **"Heavenly Father, you know exactly how I feel about that person, but I am open to you changing that."**

And it's a powerful reminder that the first prayer recorded in the Book of Mormon is Lehi praying for others and not for himself. God takes our prayers for our enemies seriously. Who knows what would have happened to Saul, turned Paul, if Stephen had never prayed for him in Acts?

Seeing through the stereotypes takes work and discipline on our part. It requires us to see every person we encounter as God sees them.

The scriptures say, *"Blessed are the merciful: for they shall obtain mercy." (Matthew 5:7)*

Why? *Because they spread it around to others.* If we are generous in one thing, let it be in mercy. May we never lose our imagination when it comes to loving people.

At the end of the day, at the end of this journey, it's about me and God. When you are offended, it helps to ask yourself these questions: Where is your heart? Your commitment? Is it on God or is it on your community?

Because even if your heart lies within your church community, that is still aligning yourself with the world, because your church community is made up of mortal men and women and they will disappoint you, even those with the best intentions. Your heart needs to transcend your community to a place where offenses are not heard and received. Jesus gives us life. The time has come to stop allowing people to rob us of the gift He has given us.

I'm afraid that I have come off like the permanent victim, as if I am always judged unfairly, but I want to tell you right now that isn't the case. I, too, sometimes judge others who seem to be different than me. I judge those who grew up in the church as shallow and boring, square, and self-absorbed. Of course, all that is completely wrong and unfair. As soon as it becomes us versus them, grace and mercy will always lose. There is not a single person sitting with you in Sacrament meeting who has it altogether—not one. No one is perfect, but God has made room for the hypocrites in His Church. People like you and me. We all fall short. We all struggle. We all are not living up to the expectations that we have set for ourselves. Everyone is in need of the tender touch of Jesus Christ in their lives.

Zion doesn't mean we will always be in harmony or some utopian fellowship; rather it's a place where we can affirm and reaffirm the truths about who we are to God. It's a place to confess our weakness and learn to extend and receive forgiveness. It's a place where we let go of our ego, and learn humility and what it's like to serve others. It's a place where we can practice loving despite the stereotypes. It's a place where God sends you someone difficult to love to help mold you into someone like Jesus, and it's where you will be that difficult person for someone to love. Sometimes we succeed, sometimes not. Sometimes we feel fulfilled, sometimes we are left empty. But, no matter what, we can be faithful within our church community. There is very little instruction in the scriptures about how to be a lone ranger while following Jesus Christ, because it was never meant to be that way. We are invited to participate in God's wedding banquet, not sit alone outside.

We need to respect the places people are at on their journey with Christ. Faith is personal. When it's interrupted by mortal people's opinions and judgments, it takes the traveler off the narrow road and brings them onto a road with barriers. Remember, *"God is more pleased with repentant sinners who are trying to draw closer to Him than with self-righteous, faultfinding individuals who, like the Pharisees and scribes of old, do not realize how badly they need to repent.*" (Elder Dale G. Renlund, *Ensign*, May 2016)

When we realize how broken we really are, it becomes a lot easier to embrace the brokenness of the people standing in front of us. I am imperfect and I'm doing the best I can, as I'm sure we all are. After that realization, it becomes easier to worship with those who reflect the image of God, but not necessarily my image.

After all, who has the perfect spouse, perfect children, or perfect parents? We do not give up on our families because they are imperfect and do not fit into our ideal expectations, so why should we give up on our ward family because they too are not fitting into the ideal? No one will ever be your ideal. No one will ever live up to your expectations. Not even you.

I had a tender mercy recently during a strip club that I Outreach to. I was invited into the dressing room to personally meet each girl and drop off homemade gifts. As soon as I walked in the room, a beautiful dancer exclaimed when she recognized me, "Hey! You're the Jesus Lady!"

The irony has not been lost on me that a stripper picked up on something I hoped to convey all along, but often got lost on people sitting next to me at church because they couldn't see past what had brought me to the feet of Christ in the first place.

We need to be kinder and gentler to one another. We need to have more compassion and love for one another. We need to show more forgiveness and mercy. We need to stop expecting a finished product out of each other while demanding grace for our own mistakes. We need to be allowed to fail without fear of judgment and ridicule. We need to build each other up in instead of tearing each other down. No one has ever felt Christ's love while being criticized. There are times for a call to repentance, but that call should only come from a place of love, and *only* from the leader who has stewardship over that person.

If I had my way, I would fill an entire ward building with those in the trenches—the heathens, the addicts, and the broken Saints. We would know right away what we were dealing with. We would know that our bishop wrestles with an addiction. Our Relief Society president feels the pains of rebellious children. My neighbor clings to her crippling marriage. A brother struggles to support his family. And I, the Woman at the Well, would sit among them. We would help *bear one another's burdens, that they may be light.* We would mourn together. We would comfort each other. We would rejoice every time one sinner came home or one Saint woke up to the goodness and freedom in Christ. We would stand as witnesses of God's encompassing light and love *at all times and in all things and in all places.* We would never journey alone. Thankfully, that is a prayer God delights in answering every Sunday morning.

If I had my way, I would fill an entire ward building with those in the trenches—the heathens, the addicts, and the broken Saints.

"We know that we have passed from death unto life, because we love [each other]. He that loveth not his brother abideth in death." (1 John 3:14)

84

8

FINALLY FINDING THE LIVING WATER

"Jesus answered and said unto her, Whosoever drinketh of this water shall thirst again: But whosoever drinketh of the water that I shall give him shall never thirst; but the water that I shall give him shall be in him a well of water springing up into everlasting life." (John 4:13–14)

THE WOMAN AT THE WELL IS SEARCHING FOR SOMETHING. SHE SEEMS to be traveling down the wrong roads looking for love, fulfillment, purpose, and meaning. When Jesus shows up on the scene, He changes everything by introducing her to a higher way of life that will never disappoint her or abandon her. He has given her hope and the chance to start over.

The first time I had an encounter with the Living Christ, it was extremely early on a cool October morning in Reno, Nevada. My husband had been deployed for a few months by this point and I had a hard time sleeping, so I decided to flip open the Book of Mormon and read through a few verses in Alma chapter 7. I have written before that when I was first baptized, I didn't have a testimony of the Book of Mormon, but on that cool morning in Reno a testimony exploded within me. The entire chapter stands as a highlight because of the amount of emotions it brought out of me that morning. It was as if Jesus, Himself, were asking me the series of questions found within the chapter, and before I could even mutter out an answer—an answer that would have been pathetic at best—He stepped inside my heart.

I felt He was literally calling my name *(see Alma 7:37)*, and no matter how far I have traveled, my name is never too far removed from His lips. That feeling of realizing that someone was out there watching over me and was deeply invested into me has been the most powerful moment of my life. All other highs, the searching for people to love and give me meaning, all the late night partying, the looking down the neck of a bottle, the abuse and neglect felt like another life. I would never need or want a new beginning because I was experiencing the ultimate new beginning sitting on my couch in the Biggest Little City. I woke up to the goodness and the truthfulness of the gospel, and my life has forever been changed by that moment. I couldn't divorce this faith even if I wanted to. It was too powerful, too deep, too personal to deny or ever walk away from. It's all true, not because I want it to be, but because it is.

We are new creatures in Christ and that is what the gospel reminds us of. Yes, there are additional blessings that come with being part of The Church of Jesus Christ of Latter-day Saints. We have a truth that no other organization has and it's brilliant all on its own. But all of those blessings are small compared to the blessing that is found in truly encountering Jesus. Every conversion, every blessing starts there. *"For God so loved the world, that he gave his only begotten Son." (John 3:16)*

When that reality is cemented in a person's heart, all other blessings take their rightful place. You'll not just seek out those blessings—such as temple sealings—because it's what everyone does, but you'll seek them out to know more about Jesus. After my encounter, there was no such thing as half in the church and half outside the church. I was all in. It was the least I could do for knowing that I was loved, wanted, and I would one day live with my Father in Heaven again.

Prior to my baptism, I had the opportunity to go on a temple tour of the Orlando Florida Temple. I thought it was absolutely the most beautiful building I had ever seen. I peeked through the glass, saw the waiting area with its white décor, and was immediately in love. Okay, with all that being said, as soon as I learned about the garments, I decided that maybe it was best to hold off on receiving my endowment. I realize how childish that sounds. Yes, everyone talks about it and how it is a wonderful experience and I believe we should strive to receive those special and sacred blessings that come with the temple, but at the time, I didn't think I was ready to give up certain things in my life so I could go.

I had those feelings until I got a calling to work with the youth teaching them the importance of family history work. I struggled with that calling. For starters, I had successfully avoided anything to do with family history up until that point. I had no idea what doing family history actually required, outside my own ignorant thought that only the elderly enjoyed doing it. Teaching family history without teaching about the temple is impossible because family history is saturated with that Holy House. I believe, without a doubt, that my family history calling is what sparked that temple fire within me.

I decided that I would start to take the necessary steps to go to the temple. I approached my bishop at a ward BBQ and nervously expressed my desire. I wanted to finally have the blessings and the power that came from being endowed. I wanted all the Church had to offer. I was ready to grow up. With my husband deployed, I was convinced that if at least one of us had the power from the temple, we would be covered the entire year. My family would remain safe. My bishop agreed and I began the process.

One of the first things I had to do was, literally clean out my closest. Very little of the clothing I owned would cover the garments that I would commit to wear after I received my endowment. Honestly, that was one of the hardest things I have had to do. I may have walked away from the party, but it still raged on in my closet. I had a hard time parting with a lot of my clothing because it felt like each piece had a story, even if the story was painful. I had to realize that I was not that clothing anymore and that I didn't belong in that clothing anymore. When God moves us from one place to another, He is moving us on to something better.

I was already experiencing this change within my heart and, with that, the desire to change my behavior seemed natural. My behavior and my heart no longer spoke in unity, and the place that God dwells was winning me over. The clothing, those halter tops and low cut shirts, may have been worn by me, but they weren't me—not the real me. God desired for me to be my best self. And with each piece of clothing I put into the black trash bag, I felt like I was letting go of an identity that was never supposed to be mine. In the end, I had a drawer full of old rocker T-shirts of some of my favorite bands and some old jeans. I felt like a weight was lifted off my shoulders. I threw the garbage bag in the car and drove it down to the nearest Salvation Army drop-off.

Next, my bishop highly suggested I attend the ward baptism night at the temple before I received my endowments. I readily agreed. Boy, I was so excited I forgot my temple name for my grandmother and other family members at my house. I had to run home to get it at the last minute. The night baptizing with my ward was the single most spiritual experience I had within the Church and it changed my life. Baptizing as proxy for my own family was incredible, particularly for my grandmother, who passed away when I was eleven years old.

Okay, so there is something you should know about me. I wear my heart on my sleeve. If I am happy, it shows all over my face and in my body language. So when I finally arrived at the temple, I was like a kid in a candy store. I had a huge smile plastered all over my face. My eyes soaked in the baptismal room. I flipped through the beautiful white scriptures as I waited. I felt this warmth invade every part of my person. My soul was ignited. All my fruitless searches for purpose and love were coming to a close. It had been almost twenty years since my grandmother slipped through the veil, and yet it felt as if she were in the room with me, filling it with her presence and encouraging me along the way.

Being baptized for her wasn't just a humbling moment, but a privilege. When it came time for me to be baptized, I broke down and sobbed in the baptismal font. I

My soul was ignited. All my fruitless searches for purpose and love were coming to a close.

actually had to take a moment to collect myself and apologize profusely. Something was happening. Something I can't explain and to try only cheapens that moment. All I know is that what I was doing at that moment made sense. For years, I looked around me and felt like I was moving without ever being part of the crowd. I felt like a stranger in my own skin. That night, I felt not only known, but loved. I had been set on fire and I felt like I couldn't contain it. I wanted more of that. I wanted to feel that love permeate my soul and my life.

I walked right out of that baptismal font and scheduled my endowment session. I would not half live this faith anymore. I would be all in. I would go the distance.

I received my endowment on December 17, 2013. The night before my endowment, Ron sat down with me and talked about the temple and bore a powerful testimony. He may never know how much that meant to me. I truly felt like I was his daughter and both he and Annette entered into that joy of going to the temple with me.

Again, I was like a wide-eyed child. I was over-the-moon excited. I soaked in my surroundings and I was grateful for the people that came to share in that moment with me. Everyone looked so beautiful dressed in white. I think that's what I loved most about the temple. Sitting there, in the middle of it, I was just like everyone else. It didn't matter the road I took to get there. It only mattered that I was there. It was a privilege and an honor to share the space with my

Latter-day family. Annette escorted me through the temple, which meant the world to me.

When the session was over and I stood among my friends and fellow Saints in the celestial room, I knew I had made the right decision, even with the garments. I knew I had finally found the family I had wanted for so long. I felt like King Lamoni:

"The dark veil of disbelief was being cast away from [her] mind, and the light which did light up [her] mind, which was the light and the glory of God, which was a marvelous light of His goodness—yea, this light had infused such joy into [her] soul, the cloud of darkness having been dispelled, and the light of everlasting life was lit up in [her] soul." (Alma 19:6)

Conversion was a slow process for me. It didn't come suddenly, but was gradual and happened almost without me knowing it. After I committed to showing up to church as myself, it was like I could finally allow God to work with me and what talents I specifically had to give Him. Often, I felt this insane amount of pressure to be perfect before I entered the temple. But after going, I realized that temple attendance is the best way to be perfected. Yes, there's a standard we need to live up to, but I think too many of us are holding ourselves back from the blessings of the temple and the living water.

The temple endows us with a certain power, but it also endows us with the courage to accept ourselves as we are and accept that we are loved and wanted by our Father in Heaven. Despite all that you have done or haven't yet done, God has been and will always be there for you. It's a promise that we can believe in.

Yes, I have done a lot of things wrong, but I have also done a lot of things right. I'm a walking paradox. I've been angry, as well as compassionate. I believe strongly. I doubt fiercely. There are areas of my life I can hand over to God and then there are some I have trouble relinquishing control. I preach hope, but behind the scenes I get discouraged and depressed. But with all that being said, we have a God who isn't afraid of our messy parts; mistakes that were made along the way neither define who we are or our true identity—they no longer control you. Only when I decided to finally let go of that pain and hurt could I really meet Jesus Christ in that place of healing and restoration. My prayer is that I am always confidently able to approach God with what He already knows about me. I am broken, but I am His.

> *"Now, it came to pass, as they went, that [Jesus] entered into a certain village: and a certain woman named Martha received him into her house. And she had a sister called Mary, which also sat at Jesus' feet, and heard his word. But Martha was cumbered about much serving, and came to him, and said, Lord, dost thou not care that my sister hath left me to serve alone? bid her therefore that she help me. And Jesus answered and said unto her, Martha, Martha, thou art careful and troubled about many things: But one thing is needful: and Mary hath chosen that good part, which shall not be taken away from her." (Luke 10:38–42)*

After my testimony started to grow, I found myself sitting in the scriptures longer, lingering after church because I wanted to, serving more fully in my calling and on my own, and I made the effort to regularly attend the temple. I didn't want to be handheld through my journey by anyone other than the Savior, Himself. Conversion will always start with the heart, extend to the hands, and hopefully through our service with the Spirit, point someone's mind toward belief. My heart changed first. Everything else has been a continuation of that.

> *"And see that ye have faith, hope, and charity, and then ye will always abound in good works." (Alma 7:24)*

God speaks into the deepest and richest part of our souls. He dares us to let go of our self-hatred, our narcissism, our insecurities, and our doubts and bring it all into His everlasting light and truth. As you convert deeper into the gospel and as you allow the Atonement to actively work in your life, refuse to allow yourself to be entertained by the exact same things Jesus went to the cross for.

A true encounter with the Living Christ will transform your life. Jesus Christ alone has the power to change you and make those changes last. Jesus is the solid foundation on whom I have rebuilt my life. The Church of Jesus Christ of Latter-day Saints is what gave me the tools. I didn't have to, but I wanted to finally lay down those "weapons of rebellion" that I had carried for so long. When I did that, when I finally gave up what was separating me from God, I not only wanted to treat others better, I started to treat myself better. *(see Mosiah 5:2)*

"[My] heart had been changed; that [I] had no more desire to do evil." (Alma 19:33)

I still worked steadfastly on my family history calling with the youth. My job was to excite the youth to work on family history. So to get the youth pumped to move forward and get inspired, I enlisted the help of the other two wards that shared my building. I turned that family history calling into a competition—whichever ward baptized and indexed the most names would win, leaving the two other wards to plan a celebration party for all the youth. Collectively, in two months, my amazing youth baptized over 1,500 names at the temple and indexed over 3,000 names in the family history database. We threw an awesome tri-ward party to celebrate.

During that time, my testimony of eternal families began to blossom into something beautiful and something I believed was finally obtainable for me. The doctrine of eternal families is a magnificent testament of the love God has for us. He gives us these relationships here in the mortal world and He doesn't let us leave here without them. It's amazing! There is no fear beyond the grave knowing who and what waits for me there. It will be a reunion like no other!

"And God shall wipe away all tears from their eyes; and there shall be no more death, neither sorrow, nor crying, neither shall there be anymore pain..." (Revelations 21:4)

I believe that this is the gospel of second chances and change. Family history provided that same opportunity of chance and change to my ancestors that had passed through the other side of the veil. I felt an undercurrent of love for my family, as broken and flawed as we are, while I worked through this calling with the youth. I began the painful process of extending forgiveness to my family as I spoke about them to the youth, and began to heal from the transgressions of my own childhood.

I started to also see my family as mortal human beings without the gospel. I understand what it's like to be lost and I know what it's like to be found. I started to understand a little more the decisions that were made and to come to terms with the abuse, the addictions, and the promiscuity. I used my own examples teaching the youth to encourage them to fill their hands with things that are noble, righteous, and worthy. "Make a difference and leave something joyous in your wake," I'd encourage them. I would remind them that what they were doing with family history was bigger—and had an eternal impact—than the small things that were placed in their day-to-day.

I started to see that impact in my own relationship with God. What I was doing for Him now was bigger than any past mistake I had ever made. I learned that God was in the business of recycling—taking our trash and turning it into treasure. Mostly, I started to see myself as a temple of God, and I had no business rooting and rolling around in places I did not belong. I am not failure free, but I am a forgivable daughter of God. My family history calling taught me that though my relationships with my family weren't anywhere I would like them to be—and they may never be in this life—in the next life I would have that relationship. The temple became the gateway to those upcoming reunions and relationships.

During this time, my life became saturated with the temple. Between my own endowment and family history calling, I began the process of preparing for my own sealing to my husband and son. Having eloped in Las Vegas, I saw the temple as an opportunity for another chance and a restart on my relationship. We started our lives together with so many problems; evil lived in full force in our relationship. I would have never thought that a temple sealing would be in our future, but Satan's best efforts were pathetic and crushed under the Atonement of Jesus Christ.

My marriage was given another start, an eternal start with God's hand lovingly guiding it. At first, I longingly flipped through Pinterest boards and dreamed of a beautiful temple sealing equipped with a reception, but we weren't rich and I needed to face the reality of it. It didn't matter anyways—the sealing blessing is still the same. The only thing that really matters when it comes to a temple sealing are the hearts that are being intertwined with God's. The rest is just fancy footwork that makes for beautiful pictures for me to "oohh" and "aahh" over on Pinterest.

The day before our sealing, my husband received his own endowment. He looked like royalty standing in the temple being escorted by our bishop. I didn't cry during my own endowment, but I cried during Alex's session. I couldn't believe this was us. Five years before, we had been drunk and wild. Three years before, we had relapsed and sworn off all religion. Once, Alex had threatened to divorce me over the Latter-day Saint religion, and now, here we were.

Despite addictions, disappointment, failures, and mistakes, we made it. His endowment was a great segue into our sealing the following day surrounded by our friends. Alex and I sat in the celestial room waiting to be brought into the sealing area just staring at each other, and I don't mean that in a romantic, melodramatic way. We started sharing stories from the first year of our marriage, "Do you remember when…?"

It was insanity to think God had brought us this far, but He had. *"With God, all things are possible," (Matthew 19:26)* and only by the grace and mercy found in the Atonement of Jesus Christ could this have ever been made possible.

We were led into the sealing room and greeted by our friends. I don't remember the prayer. I remember my bishop and Ron Perry, who were our witnesses, getting emotional. I remember Annette Perry taking her place beside me in the mother's chair. And I remember my sweet Mason being brought into the room all in white. It was the most precious moment of my life, another sweet tender mercy from my Lord and Savior.

I broke down and sobbed when Mason walked into the room. There was nothing that could have touched the tenderness of seeing him in the Lord's house, wide eyed and innocent, dressed all in white. He looked so handsome. He looked just like his father. The three of us were sealed for time and all eternity. It was powerful.

That elegant reception I wanted happened at a local BBQ joint in town. All of us dressed in our Sunday best—me in a Bohemian dress—chowing down on some ribs. It doesn't get much better than that.

Has it been "perfection" since that moment? Absolutely not. We walked out of that sealing and into a life, which is always tough. We still get in arguments, get moody, say things that are insensitive and embarrass one another in public, but our purpose has changed. I mean, God is bringing two imperfect people together and asking them to make it work, but here's the thing: God is bringing us together. There isn't just two in this marriage anymore. We aren't left to our own devices. We are being guided.

When we use flowery words and light testimonies, we give off the impression that things will always be good after a person converts, but that couldn't be further from the truth. Faithful Latter-day Saints still fail daily, experience divorce and abuse, lose money and reputation, and children go astray. God is working with mortal and broken people, not robots.

> **There was nothing that could have touched the tenderness of seeing him in the Lord's house, wide eyed and innocent, dressed all in white.**

Don't let your past, your mistakes, your failures, stop you from crossing the finish line. Work at it. Work on it. Work through it. You will make it. You can do this. Following Christ isn't easy. It's a narrow road for a reason, but it's worth it.

And with Christ, it is always infinitely better.

"The Lord works from the inside out. The world works from the outside in. The world would take people out of the slums [strip clubs]. Christ takes the slums [strip clubs] out of the people, and then they take themselves out of the slums…. the world would shape human behavior, but Christ can change human nature." –President Ezra Taft Benson (Ensign, July 1989)

9

ALABASTER OUTREACH, MY MISSIONARY OPPORTUNITY

"Behold, I say unto you, Lift up your eyes, and look on the fields; for they are white already to harvest." (John 4:35)

IF SOMEONE WOULD HAVE SAID TO ME THREE YEARS AGO THAT I WOULD be starting an outreach program for women in the sex industry, I probably would have laughed in their face. Tying my name to the industry in any way wasn't something that I would have striven for, and yet God keeps reminding me that His plans are not my plans. Following the will of God requires us to let go of our own will. We seek after His kingdom, not ours.

Alabaster Outreach was born out of the frustration and unwanted stigma that seems to be attached to people who share the similar stories as me, as well as a place of refuge for those who are hurting. One night, I was taking a walk and praying out loud my agitations after feeling like I will never fit in with the Saints. I felt alone with my story, trapped by a stereotype that I was ready to just move past. How could His people be this way? How could people be so insensitive and cruel? I couldn't believe that after all I had been through, all the changes I was making, that people could continue to only look at the surface and not see my heart. They couldn't look past what brought me to the feet of Jesus in the first place.

I openly admit my imperfections, but that doesn't make me worthless, only human. Talking openly about my past doesn't mean I continue to live within the confines of that life or that I desire to be an outsider. It's just me talking about my life. There were no words for the anger that I felt. At that moment, God answered me and definitely not in the way I expected:

"Nikki, you're right. It isn't fair; let me deal with them. But now that it has happened, what are you going to do about it? What are you going to do to make sure that never happens to another one of my daughters again?"

> **What are you going to do about it? What are you going to make sure that never happens to another one of my daughters again?"**

The scriptures say,

"In thy childhood thou hast suffered afflictions and much sorrow...Nevertheless... thou knowest the greatness of God; and he shall consecrate thine afflictions for thy gain." (2 Nephi 2:1–2)

The places of our falling may very well be the places we are called to be an agent of change and activism. God will always give us grace, wisdom, and power before He calls us. Again, I wasn't ready three years ago to reenter into the world that stole so much from me. Now, God was asking me to go back, speak up, and speak out. There are so many people whose lives are being absolutely destroyed by the lies of the industry, from those in our own homes, to those sitting beside us on Sunday mornings.

We have within us the power of Christ to make significant changes to the world around us. It's time to attack this industry that pulls in over ninety billion dollars per year. Right now, there are more strip clubs in the United States than any other country in the world.

I started Alabaster Outreach because I felt that there was a world outside the reach of the full-time missionaries that only we, the ordinary members, could impact. I also wanted to create resources within the Church where a woman coming from the background I came from could talk openly about her struggles and find hope and healing. The world is shifting into a place where promiscuity is the new normal and the people sitting in church are being affected by it. Instead of a person being judged for leaving the industry, which I have experienced, she needs to be loved and protected.

I believe most of the women within the sex industry come from a background of abuse and are looking for a place to call home and people to call family. One study suggests between sixty to ninety percent fall into that category (Farley, M. and V. Kelly, *Women and Criminal Justice,* 2000). Another study concluded that one hundred percent of exotic dancers had been physically assaulted in the clubs that they were working in, with violence that included physical assault, attempted rape, and rape (Holsopple, 1999). Another study concluded that over half (fifty-two percent) of women working as an exotic dancer have been assaulted with a weapon (Raphael & Shapiro, 2004). Eighty-nine percent of women said that if given the opportunity they would leave the industry, but feel like they are trapped with no other means for survival.

From personal experience I know that when they do leave, they will face numerous issues that will impact their physical, mental, emotional, and spiritual health. It's easy to feel desperately alone and unable to relate to anyone. Even those who want to come to church may feel like it's a waste of time and that they don't belong with God's people. I believe The Church of Jesus Christ of Latter-day Saints can provide that healing and restoration, because they did it for me.

Getting them out of the industry is just a small aspect of the Outreach. The real work will always be introducing them to a loving God and Savior. But first we have to want them more than the evil that keeps them enslaved there.

I get asked all the time what I do for Alabaster. As an Outreach, we prepare practical little gifts, things like homemade cards, feminine bath products, beauty supplies, and homemade foods for these precious sisters to let them know they are loved by God and that there is a community out there that is thinking of them. They are important and deserving of our time and we cherish them for who they are. Our goal is to empower women and foster in them a deep knowledge that they are beloved daughters of God. If they want to leave the industry, we point them in the right direction through the services that are provided by the Church. Until then, we provide friendship, prayer, and an encouraging word.

Truly, it's very simple, very anticlimactic, and very rewarding. I had a sister recently join me who was filled with trepidation, but after we went to the club and spoke to the girls, she was excited and already planning on attending the next Outreach. That's the power that comes from not only doing God's work, but doing it for the "least of these" *(see D&C 42:68).* It isn't long before you realize that we are all the "least of these" and everyone is deserving of our time and talents.

When we first started Outreaching, we were met with hesitation and very little communication, but God has opened the door to a good correspondence and openness with the girls and bouncers, and there has been nothing but friendliness ever since. My passion is these girls, shedding light on the industry, and educating the LDS community that there are people in the trenches that need to hear about the love and mercy that comes from the Atonement.

Once I read about a preacher who spoke within the prison systems. In prison, he explained, it's forbidden to smoke cigarettes and, for the most part, the only reading material available is the Bible. Though the prisoners are given Nicotine gum to help the cravings, the inmates learned that if they crushed the gum in tea leaves, they could roll it in the pages of the Bible and fashion their own cigarettes.

One day, after speaking, a prisoner approached him and said, "Pastor, I smoked Matthew. I smoked Mark. I smoked Luke. When I got to John and read how Jesus loved me, I quit."

The motivation to bring about change usually comes because of love—someone sees an offender not for who they have been, but for who they could be. The point isn't that Jesus made a Samaritan woman His first missionary, the point was that He initiated conversation with her in the first place in a culture where it was morally forbidden. Love is our devotion for God set into motion in the world around us.

It's a bold but true statement to say that Jesus never spoke to a prostitute because He had the ability to look beyond the sin and the label. He saw a daughter of God who needed to be loved standing in front of Him. He saw a woman who, somewhere along the way, someone stopped believing in her and loving her the way she needed. In the same way, I don't see a stripper when I visit these women. I see a sister and a friend. I see my own story and I know that through Jesus Christ, their ending has the possibility of being more than they could have ever imagined. We just need to introduce the gospel and leave God to do the rest. The world is dying of thirst, and though it is an overused slogan that rolls off the tongue with almost no thought anymore, it's true: Jesus is the answer to the world's drought.

Within each person we meet, we have the opportunity to see a small part of ourselves in them. If you are the spouse of a pornography addict, experienced a divorce, survivor of abuse, or an addict who is working their way through recovery, our stories and experiences are ways we can relate to one another and help each other carry what we didn't ask for and certainly didn't expect. When people share their stories with me, my first reaction is almost always, "Oh man! God is *so* going to use that testimony in the future!"

During the April, 2016, general women's session of general conference, Sister Carol M. Burton asked, "What if [that person's] story was my story?"

Most people can't even begin to imagine the horror that people have experienced and overcome in their lives. What if their story was your story? Wouldn't you want someone to come along and offer you a drink from the living water? The field is ripe for the harvest. We have a big job to do.

I can usually tell a lot about a person by the way they respond to my explanation of Alabaster Outreach. Sometimes I am met with curiosity. Most times, I am met with avoidance and hesitation. There have been times I have been criticized and judged pretty harshly.

But I have to give praise where praise is due. I am currently in a fantastic ward and stake with beautiful supporters of Alabaster Outreach and it's a tough, but needed mission. Almost a year ago, I nervously met with my stake president and explained my mission. Before I could finish the sentence, he was already invested and he has not stopped being a cheerleader for the cause.

I get asked all the time, "How do I go in these clubs and not feel any temptation?" The answer is easy. I'm not that person anymore, nor do I want to be. Gone are the days that I see the exploitation of these girls as something empowering that should be celebrated. God has taken my scattered longings and put them in their proper place. I now only see a person standing in front of me desperately wanting to know that she is loved and that she has value outside of her body. I see pain. I see abuse. I see addiction. I see brokenness. I see someone God has called me to love. I see myself, not above or below them, but someone who has walked a path, and by the grace and love of God, found a new way. I can help them carry their cross because I know the way to Calvary.

In a really strange way, it's like going back in time. I get to be the friend I always needed. That's the beauty of entering into the healing ministry of Jesus. When I'm praying for a girl in the sex industry, I'm transported back to my own days where I was morally corrupt and out of control. I feel a surge of compassion for them.

I don't understand the plans of God and often I know I am ill equipped to handle it. How He has not given up on me speaks to His divinity, not mine. He is good. I do know that everything in our lives is directional and can be used for a purpose. That has been confirmed in me over and over again.

"But the Lord knoweth all things from the beginning; wherefore, he prepareth a way to accomplish all his works among the children of men; for behold, he hath all power unto the fulfilling of all his words." *(1 Nephi 9:6)*

Blogging is fantastic and I'm grateful that I have the opportunity to do it, but all of it means nothing if I am not doing something with it. Jesus said, "Well *done*, thou good and faithful servant," not "well thought" *(see Matthew 25:21)*. We are called to share the gospel with everyone, no matter what. If Jesus could endure the cross for someone like me, I can definitely endure the little bit of uncomfortable feelings that it may take to share the gospel with someone who needs it the most. Everyone matters, not just those who show up at church on Sundays.

"The sheep is worthy of divine rescue simply because it is loved by the Good Shepherd...It matters not how you became lost—whether because of your own poor choices or because of circumstances beyond your control. What matters is that you are His child. And He loves you. He loves His children." President Dieter F. Uchtdorf (Ensign, May 2016)

That is a promise we can cling to. God loves His children. Period. No additional information is required.

10

DIVING IN HEAD FIRST

" Jesus saith unto them, My meat is to do the will of him that sent me, and to finish his work." (John 4:34)

WHEN YOU COLLIDE WITH JESUS, YOU LEARN THAT BEATING AROUND the bush is no longer acceptable by Him. You are either in or you are out. There can be no in between. There comes a point in everyone's path toward true faith that a decision has to be made. Will I sit on the bank or will I dive into the stream of God's love and will for my life? Will I, like Lehi, follow the command to leave everything I know to journey into the wilderness?

When I finally decided to dive into the living water, that intense love and acceptance from my Father in Heaven and Jesus Christ washed over and through me. I realized that what I had to bring to the kingdom with my broken past was enough. God could work with it and I was willing to let Him.

Admittedly, I am a sinner. If you're looking for perfection, you will be disappointed by me. I walk a fine line between faith and doubt. Sometimes all I can muster is the basic foundation of faith, and sometimes I feel like I can move mountains. Being a member of The Church of Jesus Christ of Latter-day Saints goes against everything I had ever known or done. I am a shattered woman with a damaged past, but it's through that brokenness that light is able to shine through and illuminate the path in front of me.

I am not a flawless daughter of God, but I am a forgivable

daughter of my Heavenly Father. And I have to keep reminding myself of that daily.

Recently, my family and I had the opportunity to visit Salt Lake City for the very first time, so of course we made our way to Temple Square! I had one goal—I wanted to see the famous marble statue of Jesus, the Christus. When we walked to the visitor's center, there were a couple people there talking to the missionaries, so we were able to make our way to the front to get a better view of the statue.

My focus was on the scars that were etched on Jesus' hands and feet. There is so much beauty, grace, and mercy found in those wounds. Our salvation has come by a crimson-stained hand, and we have so much to be grateful for. There is power at the feet of Jesus. There is strength and healing. Not a single person sitting in church with you will make it unless they first go to the cross with Jesus.

Everyone is struggling. Everyone in some capacity is broken, but because of the Atonement, we are not broken beyond repair. God's grace and mercy can be found everywhere, and I am a witness to that.

"For we are his workmanship, created in Christ Jesus." (Ephesians 2:10)

There are so many Saints that may feel like they are drowning under life's pressures and fighting to stay afloat, but you are not alone on this journey. We are not meant to travel alone, and yet we opt to hide our true selves and struggles, which only leave us feeling as if we are the most broken person in the room. I promise you, you are not. I receive emails all the time from people bravely sharing their stories with me. I want so badly to put everyone in the same room and just tell them to talk it out, because so many of us are wrestling the same demons. We are here to help each other and to strengthen one another, and we can't do that if we are too busy trying to outrun one another.

Life isn't fair. Bad things happen to good people. Good things happen to bad people. Marriages end in divorce. People who desperately want children learn they are barren. No, life is not fair. But God is not life, and if we confuse God with life, we are setting ourselves up for serious disappointment and heartache. God never promised deliverance from hardships and struggles—even His own Son wasn't immune to them—but He not only promised that He would help us in the middle of our burdens, but that He would use our burdens to glorify Him.

"And I will also ease the burdens which are put upon your shoulders, that even you cannot feel them upon your backs, even while you are in bondage; and this will I do that ye may stand as witnesses for me hereafter, and that ye may know of a surety that I, the Lord God, do visit my people in their afflictions." (Mosiah 24:14)

Despite it all, God has been really good to me. I have been asked once if given the opportunity to change anything in my life, would I? And my answer is no, I wouldn't. Certainly, it has not been easy, but it helped me encounter God. I've done both living in the world and living for God, and hands down I have been more fulfilled and joyous living in the presence of God than in the world.

Everything, absolutely everything, in my life has pointed me to God, even the bad. You have not lost value because you made a mistake. God can use all your mistakes and failures to bring Him Glory and further His kingdom, if we let Him. But first we have to give it all to Him.

I realized that I was harboring so much anger at my past, and like the Lamanites, was letting it destroy me from the inside out. The first step was realizing that even though a lot of my decisions were within my control, a lot of them were not, but *all* of them happened with the eyes of Heaven. God suffers *with* us. What hurts us, hurts Him. And God has the ability to turn those messy places into beautiful spaces.

> **I've done both living in the world and living for God, and hands down I have been more fulfilled and joyous living in the presence of God than in the world.**

Satan will want you to think otherwise. He wants you to stay in those past mistakes and transgressions. He wants you to believe that you are too far gone, too hopeless, and too worthless. Satan's greatest weapon will always be psychological. If He can get you to doubt God and Jesus Christ, doubt the gospel, and doubt that you are truly a Child of God, we can't effectively fight against him. If we keep fighting against ourselves, beating ourselves up, we will have nothing left to stand against him, the real enemy. Satan only wins if we quit trying and stop believing in Jesus.

It is God's will that His people move forward to build up His kingdom. It's is God's will that we know that we are not only loved, but really liked by Him. It's God's will that we strengthen one another with our testimonies and stories. It's God's will that He is glorified in our daily interactions. There is a gospel to preach. There are people to love. There are wounds to bind up and addictions to be conquered. We're not waiting for God's approval or proof to move forward and make a change. We are that proof! We are His Church!

Can you, beloved reader, accept that you are accepted by God not as you think you should be, but as you are—with all of your baggage and mistakes? You do not need to be perfect to love others and you certainly don't need to be perfect to share the gospel. Look at the people Christ surrounded himself with—He purposely chose the *"the foolish things of the world to confound the wise; and God hath chosen the weak things of the world to confound the things which are mighty." (1 Corinthians 1:27)*

I wrote this book for the heathens, the outcasts, and the least of these. I wrote this for those trying to find the Way, the Truth and the Light in a world that is screaming at us through a megaphone that we are always wrong. I wrote this book for those that are tired and thirsty walking the dusty roads of Samaria; I wrote this for people like myself. There is nothing that you have ever done that God can't use to further His kingdom. No matter where you are on this journey, with Christ there is always a chance to start over and begin again. We serve a God who not only says, "Come and follow me," but also says, "Come back. You have a place here." For anyone who thinks God only works through the perfected Saints, I hope my story offers encouragement. God works through real people. The best thing we have is our testimonies of a changed life through our Lord and Savior.

I uprooted myself from a life I knew and thought I loved. I lost friends, family, and almost my marriage because of my membership within the Church. I have been misjudged, labeled, and hurt. And every single temptation that I have struggled with has still manifested itself in my life. So *has* it been worth it? Absolutely yes. I'd do it all over again if it meant that I could collide with Jesus in the exact same way. It's been a tough journey, but a good one.

Yes, this gospel is for you, the broken and the hurting. It is your opportunity for a second chance. That change you have always wanted is here. If God can take a sinner like me and turn her into a Saint, He can do anything.

My name is Nikki. I am a Latter-day Woman at the Well, and I have found the living water. I am His witness that you can find it too.

ACKNOWLEDGMENTS

THIS IS THE BOOK THAT SHOULD HAVE NEVER HAPPENED; YET, GOD HAS been so good to me. Everything that I thought I wanted, God has given me the exact opposite and proven to me that my ways are not His, and His ways are infinitely better. My life is one of gratitude and devotion to Jesus Christ and Heavenly Father. My thank you will forever be to Him first. Thank you, Jesus, for everything that led me to know you. I'd do it all over again if it meant I could come to know You in the exact same way.

To my husband, my eternal companion: thank you for loving me through it all, for never clipping my wings, and for allowing me the room to grow into the woman God wants me to be. Thank you for being my safe place to land when I've jumped beyond myself. For being my comedian, my shoulder, my secret keeper and dreamer. Eternity is so much sweeter knowing you are with me.

To my son: you and only you gave me the title I am proudest of, "mom." This book is for you.

Thank you Russell and Shelley Stoddard for believing in me and believing me. Thank you for your acceptance and looking past the label. Thank you for encouraging me to become a woman undone and allow myself to be put back together by Jesus Christ. And Russ, thanks for not letting me quit on that youth challenge. It was the most stressful and tiring thing I have ever done, and it sealed the deal with my testimony. Thank you for being my bishop, for knowing when to push, when to back off, when to speak up and out and knowing what I needed before I did.

Ron and Annette Perry: Thank you for giving me the LDS family I always wanted and showing me what it feels like to be apart of something bigger than myself. Your love was tangible and real. With you, I belonged.

To my amazing publishing company, Snowy Peaks Media, thank you for taking a chance on an unknown former stripper who wrote a blog. Thank you for empowering me and my story, and for being patient and respectful to my journey. Heather Godfrey, thanks for letting me text you all the time with all my goofy concerns and jokes.

To my Hillcrest Ward, I adore all you crazy, eclectic people for God. What an incredible ward to be a part of for this season in my life. I couldn't have asked for a better community to share in this joy. This is scary, but it's a little less scary with you.

To my Pyramid Lake Ward: thanks for allowing me the opportunity to bloom.

Beth and Moroni, thanks for letting me vent and cry it out to you. Wherever I was in this journey, you were right there to let me talk it out and for the added perspective. We have years of friendship behind us and many more before us. Cheers to the years to come.

To the reader: thank you for taking this journey with me, for allowing me to come into your home and heart with my story. From my heart to yours, Jesus is the answer.

ABOUT THE AUTHOR

A NATIVE TO FLORIDA, NIKKI YASTE CURRENTLY LIVES IN NORTHERN California with her husband, Alex, who is currently serving active duty in the Air Force, and their son, Mason. They were sealed as a family in the Reno Nevada Temple in 2014.

In her small corner of the internet, Nikki is known as the LDS Woman at the Well. She is a blogger and speaker and is passionate about blogging her journey with Jesus. Her desire is to reach those that may feel they don't have a place within their community and who struggle to accept that God loves them right where they are.

Nikki is the founder of Alabaster Outreach, a ministry currently serving women working within the sex industry in Northern California. She believes that there is no one beyond the grace and mercy of God and that everyone deserves to know that truth.

When there is time, Nikki is an avid runner and yogini. You can usually find her browsing used bookstores and buying old records.